GLIMPSES OF INDIA

AND OF

MISSION LIFE

GLIMPSES OF INDIA

AND OF

MISSION LIFE

MRS. HUTCHEON

GYAN

Published by

Gyan Publishing House
5, Ansari Road
Daryaganj, New Delhi-110002
Phone: 011-47034999, 9811692060
E-mail: books@gyanbooks.com

Distribution Network
gyanbooks.com
India, USA, Canada, UK, Australia

ISBN: 978-93-6780-321-9 (PB)

First Published, 1878

2nd Impression 2024

Printed at: Gyan Press, Delhi.

GLIMPSES OF INDIA AND OF MISSION LIFE
Author: MRS. HUTCHEON

THE MUSSULMAN MOHARAM.

GLIMPSES OF INDIA

AND OF

MISSION LIFE.

BY

MRS. HUTCHEON.

AUTHOR OF 'LIGHT AMID THE SHADOWS,' &c.

London:

PUBLISHED FOR THE AUTHOR AT THE

WESLEYAN CONFERENCE OFFICE,

2, CASTLE-STREET, CITY-ROAD;

AND 66, PATERNOSTER-ROW.

1878.

PREFACE.

No one who has felt the burden of India's salvation can ever cast off that burden. The writer of GLIMPSES has had a deep sense of this responsibility. For many years, hard and practical Mission work was the joy and inspiration of her life. Ever since loss of health drove her from the field itself, and prevented much personal labour, she has felt that she still owed a debt to India. This book is part of the payment of that debt.

There is a large amount of personal narrative in this Missionary book. But this is not to glorify self. The writer's natural modesty would lead her to shrink from publicity. Her grand motive has been to awaken and feed an intelligent interest in Mission work, and to call out more effort and self-denial in behalf of the perishing millions of India. This she has tried to do by describing such facts, and by giving such correct and lifelike pictures, as could only be the result of personal observation and experience.

The morning has dawned; the light is spreading.

The future of India is as bright as prophecy and promise, and as sure as the Father's gift to His Son. But before the perfect day of India's salvation has come, the Church must continue the work of faith, the labour of love, and submit to the patience of hope. Many of her best sons must be sent to India and buried there. Much more wealth must be expended there. The spirit of the Cross must be more deeply felt, and its grand law of self-denial be more fully exercised.

We commend this little book to the friends of Missions, and invoke upon its story the blessing of Jesus, the world's great Missionary.

JOHN HUTCHEON.

THE MANSE, GREEN LANES, LONDON.
November 8th, 1878.

CONTENTS.

Chapter I.

FIRST IMPRESSIONS.

The Sea—First Indian Home—The Old Munshi—Scenes at the Moharam—Our Cook's Holiday—My First Pupil—Timothy's Story—First View of Idolatry—The Dasari Feast—Caste of India—Our Native Students—Athasheshalu—His Death . . . . . . Pages 1—22

Chapter II.

MYSORE—THE BATTLE AND THE VICTORY OF FEMALE EDUCATION.

Proverbs about Female Education—First Pariah Pupils—A Bitter Disappointment—The Priest's Anger—Little Lingi—First Girls' School in the Pettah—Early Lessons—The Sick Scholar and the Charm—An Unnecessary Burden—English Dolls—Timmi's Conversion—Encouragements—The Runaway—The Mother's Vow—The False Alarm—A School in the Palace—Farewell to Girls' Schools . . . . 23—43

Chapter III.

A TOUR IN THE REGIONS BEYOND.

Among Thieves—Preparations for Tour—The Midnight Attack—Shravana Balagola—The Missionary Caught—The Jaina Swàmi—Scenes at Hassan—The Dying Brahman's wish—A Hindu's Idea of Happiness—A Novel Highway—The Halabede Temple—A Noble Banyan—The Village Festival—Measuring Swords—An Elfin Nook—The Benkipoor Tiger . . . . 44—68

Chapter IV.

THE NUGGAR JUNGLES AND FALLS OF GAIRSAPPA.

Loveliness of the Forest—A Strange Night—First Glimpse of Sheràvutty—Crossing the River—Leeches—The Falls—Descent to the Bottom—A Providential Escape—The Falls of Gairsappa . . . . . . 69—80

Chapter V.

FIRST FRUITS GATHERED IN MYSORE.

Our New Station—Its Labourers—Yeeranagerry—Blighted Hopes—Our First Converts—Dévadetta Slippered by his Father—Stephen's Noble Confession—Persecution—A Wonderful Trophy—Shanta's Fiery Ordeal—The Panchàyat—A Ludicrous Incident—Jivawashanu—His Death and Funeral—Effects produced in the Village 81—98

Chapter VI.

THE BLUE MOUNTAINS.

Tipacardu Jungle—Midnight Ride through the Forest—The Mountain Pass—Glories of the Mountain Land—A Soldiers' Love-feast—Our Nest among the Hills—Botany of the Nielgherries—The Todas—Their Marriage Ceremony—A Severe Trial—Reunion—The Forest Warblers . . . . 99—113

Chapter VII.

SMALLER TENANTS OF THE MISSION COMPOUND.

Mosquitoes—Insect Gems—Black, Red, and White Ants—Missionary driven from his Room—Soap-nut Tree—A Thief Caught—Musk Rats—Snakes—Cobra's Fangs Extracted—A Memorable Evening—Tricks of the Monkeys . . . . 114—127

Chapter VIII.

DARK DAYS IN MISSION LIFE.

The Swinging Feast—The Great Tank—Days of Drought—The Rain-maker—Feeding the Hungry—A Breathing Skeleton—Days of Terror—The Widow's only Son—Setting in of the Monsoon . . . . . . 128—140

Chapter IX.

THE NATIVE COURT OF MYSORE.

Four Palaces—The Rajah—Our First Visit—Royal Captives—Indian Procession—Durbar—A Dazzling Scene—Presentation of Gifts from Queen Victoria—A Silver Shower—Last Visit to the Rajah—Dying Days—His Death—The Funeral Procession—Burning . . 141—154

Chapter X.

THE SACRED SHRINE.

Nunjingode—A Brahmani Lady—Hindu Widow—The Temple—Scene in the Courtyard—The Pilgrims—Their Penances—Child's First Lesson in Idol Worship—Scene by the River—A Touching Incident—Lost on Mount Wellington . . . . 155—167

Chapter XI.

A SANCTUARY TO THE CHRISTIANS' GOD.

The Street Preacher—The Cruel Taunt—Jubilee Festival—Old John's Offering—A Sad Disappointment—Christmas Morning—Laying Foundation Stone—The Entertainment—Erection of Chapel—Remarks of the Heathen—Opening Services—Old John's Legacy—Ten Years' Prayer Answered . . . . 168—177

Chapter XII.

PEEPS INTO HINDU HOMES.

Invitation to Zenana—Interior of Native House—Hindu Ladies—Dress and Jewels—Another Hindu Home—A Baby dressed in Jewels—A Holy Man—A Rare Compliment—The Young Widow—Native Family Festival—Two Little Brides—Curiosities of Native Etiquette—Cruel Treatment of Females—Occupation of Hindu Ladies—Woman's Power—Simple Faith—Three Noble Sisters—St. Helena's Two Graves . . . . 178—200

LIST OF ILLUSTRATIONS.

PAGE

THE MUSSULMAN MOHARAM (*Frontispiece*).

SHRAVANA BALAGOLA 44

THE FALLS OF GAIRSAPPA 69

THE NIELGHERRY TRIBES 99

SNAKE CHARMERS 114

THE RAJAH OF MYSORE 141

THE NUNJINGODE TEMPLE 155

THE NATIVE CHAPEL, MYSORE 168

THE SEA.

THE sea, the sea, the beautiful sea,
Bounding along in its gladness free;
Never at rest, for it cannot stay,
Laughing and dancing in joyous play;
Catching each tint of the sunset sky,
Its purple crimson and azure dye;
Each wavelet crowned with a golden gleam,
Fading away like a blissful dream.
A thing of transcendent purity,
Art thou, O beautiful sunlit sea.

The sea, the sea, the all-circling sea,
Stretching its billows so mightily;
Clasping together with silver band
Earth's severed races, each zone and land,
From ice-bound shores of eternal snow
To sunny climes where the palm trees grow,
Wreathing full many an island gem
Around thy brow like a diadem;
Chanting thy chorus through coral halls
With fluted pillars and rainbow walls;
Laving sad realms of disease and death,
Fanning hot brows with thy healing breath,
Yet bearing no taint away on thee,
Thou world-encircling, kingly sea.

The sea, the sea, the tempest-tossed sea,
So fearful yet full of majesty;
Rearing its billows like mountains high,
Seething and gurgling with hollow cry;
Digging a yawning, mysterious grave
Within its depths for the seaman brave;
And hiding the young, the loved, the fair,
'Mong its shells and pearls and treasures rare;

Prancing along like a war-horse proud,
Snorting defiance to wind and cloud,
Shaking the earth with its revelry,
A thing of dread is the storm-tossed sea!

The sea, the sea, the fathomless sea,
Teeming with life though thy waters be;
Vast and unmeted by human hand,
Obedient thou to thy God's command.
He set the bounds which thy proud waves know,
And rules thy tides in their ebb and flow.
In that grand new earth we hope to see,
Where to live is immortality,
God's love like a mighty ocean wide
Shall leave no room for thy swelling tide.
No people of diverse tongue and race
Inhabit that holy dwelling-place;
Their castes they leave with the flesh behind,
And, all united in heart and mind,
They speak one language and breathe one air,
In that holy region pure and fair;
One song shall sing through the endless years,
When hushed the music of yonder spheres;
And heard no more shall the thunders be
Of thy grand anthem, tremendous sea!

GLIMPSES OF INDIA AND MISSION LIFE.

CHAPTER I.

PART I.—FIRST IMPRESSIONS.

INDIA at last! All faces gather brightness, for the swellings and calms of old ocean are now to be numbered among memories of the past.

At daybreak, June 5th, 1860, the oft-pictured shore, with its palm trees, minarets, and pagodas, stretches full in view. One other brief ordeal in crossing the wild-roaring Madras surf, then a journey of two days and two nights, amid strange scenes and new experiences, and our destination is reached. Bangalore, that sounding name, which had echoed even in our dreams, is at length a reality. Yes; but very different from all the Bangalores seen in dreamland.

Our first Indian home was a neat little bungalow in the large Mission compound, at the end of which stood our Anglo-Vernacular Institution for native youths, and also the printing-press. On either side were the residences of Missionaries, our nearest neighbours being our dear friends, Mr. and Mrs. Sanderson. It was a bright and cheerful beginning to our Missionary career; for Bangalore is by no means a purely native station such as Mysore, our next more trying but deeply interesting one, was. Here we could enjoy blessed communion with other Christians, and delightful religious services in our own tongue.

I arrived in India at a happy time. The mutiny was crushed, the tumultuous throbbings of the great pulse of the nation had subsided, and peace reigned in our borders. Bangalore is an important military station, and it was then our privilege to meet with not a few British officers, of whom any country might well be proud. Heroes they were in every sense of the word, good soldiers, not only of our beloved Queen, but also of the Lord Jesus. It was refreshing indeed, to hear their mighty prayers and soul-stirring appeals at our weekly meetings. But even in this favoured spot, most of our surroundings reminded us that we were dwellers in a foreign land, and, sadder still, a land wholly given to idolatry.

Just outside the Mission compound lay the entrance to the *pettah*, or native town. All along the crowded streets, over the flat-roofed, mud-walled houses, waved rows of the stately cocoa-nut tree. Leaping among these, and on every house-top, wall, and verandah, a crowd of chattering, grinning, defiant monkeys ever held themselves in readiness to pounce on the first prize, which their daring or cunning could manage to secure. That they were a terror and trouble to every householder, the natives would freely own; but then, the monkey is one of their gods, so these wrongs could find no redress.

With what interest did we watch the dark faces

around us. There were the women in their long, bright *sheerès,* or flowing cloth, with their babies mounted on their sides, and their baskets or waterpots nicely poised on their heads. We loved to study the intelligent countenances of the turbaned figures, too,—men so shrewd and clever in all their undertakings, that it was hard to believe that such could ever bow down to gods of wood and stone. But what mark is that on every forehead? On some there is a white and yellow trident, and on others long horizontal stripes, with a circular spot in the centre. Alas! they tell us that these are the worshippers of Vishnu and of Shiva.

But my heart yearned with peculiar tenderness over the dark-eyed women, who came shyly peeping through the glass door and open windows of our bungalow, to catch a glimpse of the 'new *dhori-sani.*' They were our native Christians, and I longed, oh so much, to talk with them; but I could only acknowledge their greetings by returning their polite salaams and by smiling upon them. As yet there yawned a great chasm between us: I knew not their language, and they knew nothing of mine.

The old *munshi,* of whom so correct a likeness is given in Mr. Hodson's interesting memoir of *Old Daniel,* was one of our first native visitors. Through his precious spectacles, the much valued gift of his former talented pupil, the Rev. William Arthur, the old man scanned me closely from head to foot. What his private conclusion might be he prudently kept to himself, but noticing the deep blush that rose under his scrutinising gaze, he politely turned it off—as a Hindu knows so well how to do—by saying, 'As the new moon, when she arises is the desire of all eyes, so is the young

English *dhori-sani,* who has but newly appeared among us.' That *munshi* was a general favourite in the Mission. He knew no English whatever, but he was a clever man, and an able Canarese teacher. He had a happy, genial disposition, with a vein of ready wit and sparkling humour. Though on his brow he wore the badge of idolatry, yet in the quiet of the study he repeatedly owned his entire belief in the great truths of Christianity. When, a few years after, we visited Bangalore again, and I was able to converse with him in Canarese, he would speak so feelingly of the Lord Jesus, that we felt sure he was not far from the kingdom of God.

Once we were reading together the touching story of the Saviour's condescension and love in washing the disciples' feet. The face of the old *munshi* manifested unusual emotion, and he asked, 'Why did Peter exclaim, "Lord, not my feet only, but also my hands and my head"?' I replied, that, 'if submission to this act were necessary in order that the disciples should have a part with Christ, warm-hearted Peter must have the very fullest share.' 'No,' said the aged idolater; 'I think it was this: to wash the feet only, is the work of the lowest servant in the house, but the father and the mother will pour water on the hands and on the head. Peter loved his Master so much, that he could not be satisfied if Jesus were less to him than his father, his mother, his all.' It was an Eastern's familiar rendering of this beautiful narrative, which in its sublime significance had deeply touched the old man's heart.

I had been but a few weeks in India, when I had such a view of the power of fanaticism and superstition over its votaries, as long years that have rolled away since then have not yet effaced. It was the great Mahomedan yearly festival, the Moharam. My husband, who had already been four years in the country, wished me to form a correct estimate at the beginning of my Missionary career, of the various foes with which we have to measure swords on that trying battlefield. So, early one afternoon, we drove through the *pettah*, while that degrading feast was in full play.

In many places light booths had been erected for the occasion, festooned by the pale-green, giant leaves of the banana. Inside them were placed exquisite little models of Mahomedan mosques and minarets, all sparkling with gold and imitation gems. Though these were chiefly formed of rice-paper, muslin, and other flimsy materials, the effect was exceedingly good, and the workmanship most ingenious. Every available house-top, nook, and corner of the principal thoroughfares were crowded by an eager, excited mass of spectators. Hindus were there in thousands as well as Mussulmans, all in their brightest holiday dress. The women and children were gaily adorned with flowers and jewels.

But on entering the main street of the *pettah*, the scene of mad revelry which burst upon us baffles all description. Men wearing the skins of tigers, bears, leopards, and other wild animals, some representing fierce birds of prey, and many hideous figures with masks and horns dressed up as devils, closed round our conveyance on every side. They howled, yelled, and tumbled in the dust, rolling over and over. Then they would leap, dance, fight, and drag each other about, till we were fain to close both eyes and ears. The people seemed quite mad with excitement and folly, and almost crawled among our horse's feet. All seemed bent on trying who could most completely deface the noble image in which God created man. A few bold fellows held up large birds close to our faces in their wild merriment; and thankful indeed was I to escape away to the quiet of green fields again. There one could at least shut out such sights and sounds, though the painful impress of them will ever remain in our hearts.

But this was not all. The Moharam lasts for ten days and ten nights, and during the whole of this time, intense excitement prevails. The men dig pits in the roads, and at nightfall great fires are kindled in them. Through these they madly leap and dance in large groups. They then repair to the various mosques, where they sit listening to pathetic tales of the two hero-brothers, Hassan and Hoosein. When they come to the tragic account of their sufferings and death, the Mussulmans weep and beat their heads and breasts, till, towards morning, many of them sink on the ground in sheer exhaustion.

Once at the commencement of this degrading feast, our cook presented himself with a profound salaam, and said, 'Missus, please give leave for two days?'

'Why, Poonoswammy? what do you want a holiday for?'

'Little sick, ma'am; just now medicine never drinking, then plenty sick soon coming.'

'Very well, you may rest for two days.'

However, before the sick man returned, a Christian servant came and asked, 'Does Missus know that Poonoswammy is playing tiger at the Moharam?' So in future we took care that our tiger should be chained at such times, whether well or ill.

Many of our friends at home will be surprised to learn that there are nearly twice as many Mahomedans in India alone, as there are in all the Turkish empire. While in the latter they number fifteen or sixteen millions, in Hindustan they are estimated at thirty millions. The higher classes of these are descendants of the officials and great men, who in the days of Mahomedan ascendency received large government pensions. They never became landed proprietors, and their children have gradually been sinking down into poverty and obscurity. The Hindus have far outstripped them in the march of education, for out of the twenty-one millions in Bengal only twenty-eight thousand Mahomedans attended government schools, according to recent statistics.

As yet little has been done for these by Christian Missions. But if we have seen it needful to despoil them of political power, and to take the sword from the oppressing hand of the Moslem, can it be less the duty of our nation now to offer them freely the blessed Gospel of peace? By whom are the pure and holy precepts of the religion of Jesus more urgently needed, than by the cruel and fanatical followers of the false prophet?

Comparatively few as their opportunities have been to those of the Hindu, yet, strange to say, my first pupil in India was a young Mahomedan. His baptism was the first of a native convert I ever witnessed in India. One day, a few weeks after the Moharam, while seated at work in the study, the door opened, and Daniel, our catechist, with a respectable young Mussulman, entered. After a few words of introduction and welcome, the stranger told his simple tale in a voice tremulous with emotion. Zoolfakar Hoosein, was the only and beloved son of a Mahomedan doctor in Madras. He had often heard the name of Jesus, and though he knew but imperfectly the story of His love, it had haunted his spirit. Secretly he already felt something of its sweetness and strange power. In the month of July, 1860, cholera broke out in Madras, and raged with terrible severity all around Triplicene, the Mahomedan quarter. Zoolfakar was himself smitten, and appeared to be dying. Conscience, partially aroused before, now awoke him fully to the dread reality of his position. In the anguish of his soul, he felt that the faith of his people had no anchorage that would hold good in such an hour.

He now turned his despairing eye to the Christian's refuge, and vowed that, if God would in pity hear his cry and spare his life, he would become a true follower of the Lord Jesus. His prayer was heard, and he at once began to recover. His anxiety next was, how his vow could best be performed. Zoolfakar knew well that his father, a proud and bigoted Mahomedan, would violently oppose, and if possible prevent, the solemn step from being taken. He therefore expressed a strong desire to visit Bangalore, where several of his relatives resided. Thinking that the health of her son needed change, his mother readily gave her consent, little dreaming of all that was to follow; and he at once proceeded thither.

The young inquirer soon found out our catechist, Daniel, and to him he unburdened his full heart. At the same time, he eagerly asked for further instruction in the great truths and duties of Christianity, to all of which he listened most earnestly. It was at this stage that he was first brought to the Missionary, and many an interesting interview they had together. At length when Zoolfakar's sincerity had been fully tested, my husband one day asked him:

'Why are you so wishful to be baptized at once?'

'Oh, Sir,' replied the youth, 'my brother-in-law found me reading a gospel a few days ago, and in his rage he compelled me to accompany him to the mosque, where I was beaten. I fear he will lay violent hands upon me, and I want to be baptized before I die.'

'Have you no other reason for desiring baptism?' he was asked.

'No, Sir,' earnestly answered Zoolfakar; 'I only want to save my soul, and confess Christ, then they may do what they will with my body.'

Sabbath morning came, when, with his countenance beaming with holy joy, he knelt, and in the presence of our native Church received the name of Timothy Zoolfakar.

The storm of persecution now burst upon the young convert in all its fury. He was pointed at, mocked, spit upon, and openly reviled by his relatives and friends in Bangalore. Tidings soon reached Madras, and his infuriated father at once publicly disowned his son. He at the same time thrust the mother out of doors, because she had first consented to the youth's visiting his sister. Poor Timothy felt this to be a bitter cup indeed. He loved his mother, and the thought that she must suffer for his sake was a painful trial. But he had long since counted the cost, and now patiently strove to endure all for the sake of Jesus. One day, about this time, he received a letter from his father, threatening him with personal violence when they met.

The old man went on to say, that as he could no longer show his face in public on account of the disgrace brought upon him by his son, he was about to proceed to Mecca on pilgrimage.

As Timothy appeared to be intelligent, and was most anxious to pursue his studies, we took him under our protection, and he was admitted as a Christian student into our English institution. In order to help him to surmount his first difficulties there, I taught him privately for an hour each day, and he seemed deeply grateful for this little kindness. Often with a kindling eye he would say, 'There are many Missionaries to the Canarese and Tamul people, but who preaches of Jesus to mine? If I live, by God's help, I *must* teach my own people.'

One day in the month of November, Timothy came to us trembling exceedingly. He held in his hand an open letter, which he had just received, professedly, from his mother. It informed him that his father was now dead, that she wept day and night with longing to see the face of her son again, and that he must hasten to her immediately. If he remained away, and refused to grant her request, then the distress and ruin which he had already brought upon the family would be complete. As he read all this to us, poor Timothy shook from head to foot, and wept bitterly. It was hard indeed for an only son to break his mother's heart. But we had strong reasons for believing this letter to be but a wicked stratagem to lead the youth to place himself in the power of his cruel father. So we persuaded him on no account to regard it.

At the Christmas holidays, however, his desire to see and to cheer the heart of the poor mother who still fondly loved him, became so intense, that we could no longer restrain Timothy from taking the journey.

'I will comfort her, tell her everything, and at once return,' he said. 'Was it not by my own deliberate choice and conviction that I left all and became a Christian? What motive could now induce me to waver or turn back?' We trembled when, like another warm-hearted but weak disciple, we heard him say, 'Though all should forsake Christ, yet will I never.' We warned him of his frailty, and of the danger to which he was exposing himself; and commending him to the special protection of God, we sorrowfully said good-bye for a time. Long we watched and hoped for his return, but, alas! we saw his face no more. What the fate of poor Timothy was, whether he fell a victim to the cruel and fanatical zeal of his people, or whether, like Peter, he denied his Lord, we shall probably never know till the dawn of that day, when the secrets of all hearts shall be revealed.

PART II.—FIRST VIEW OF IDOLATRY.

OUR hearts had just been gladdened by the baptism of Timothy Zoolfakar, and the hopes that had centred in our first Mahomedan convert were yet high, when, in one day, I had such a view of popular idolatry as might well have sufficed for a lifetime. We have seen it in most of its aspects and phases since then, from the rude and disgusting mud image of the simple village idolater, to the proud idol procession, surrounded by all the *éclat* and pageantry of a lavish

Eastern court. But never, perhaps, was I so stunned and distressed as by that first great view of idolatry on the wide *meidan*, or plain, just outside Bangalore. It was the most important of all the Hindu yearly festivals, the Dassara, which, like the Moharam of the Mahomedans, continues for ten days.

At the conclusion of this feast, every implement of use and industry is brought out, and worshipped by its owner. The writer prostrates himself before his pen, the scholar his book, the farmer his plough, the tailor his needle, and the carpenter his tools. The sacred animals, too, come in for their share in the general adoration. Then, after mid-day, all the principal temple and household gods are brought out, and paraded with great pomp on the high, open ground before named.

I seem to see it all before me now, as the sad exhibition burst upon us eighteen years ago. The excited tens of thousands were there again. Old men with stooping gait and silvery locks, men in the glory of their prime, laughing youths, and wondering little children; grandmothers, too, and comely, jewelled matrons, with their pretty infants and graceful daughters, vied with each other in worshipping the gods fashioned by human hands. These idols were of every conceivable size, shape, and device. This will excite no surprise if we remember that India can boast of her three hundred and thirty millions of gods!

What a collection of deities met our eye on every side! Idols of gold and idols of silver, of brass also, of wood, and of stone. Some were hideous and disgusting, some grotesque, more altogether meaningless; but each and all had their adoring votaries. The larger and heavier idols were borne along on platforms, richly festooned with flowers, and hung with crimson drapery. Over the heads of the gods, rainbow-coloured canopies, or umbrellas with gold fringe, were held. Many gaily decorated idols were slowly carried about in showy, gilded palanquins. Bands of native musicians marched before the principal gods, and bearers waved in one hand their flaming torches, while in the other each held his long-necked cruse of oil, with which, from time to time, he fed the flame. White clouds of incense rose to the sky from the censers of many priests; and dancing girls, loaded with jewels—without whom no temple or procession in India would be deemed complete,—sang, gestured, and made rapid evolutions around the idols. As the various pageants passed through the admiring multitudes, they shouted, clasped their hands, and made lowly obeisance to the gods.

The numerous and constantly recurring Hindu feasts form the very life of popular idolatry. The sympathy of vast numbers, and the intense excitement of so many religious holidays, alone save it from becoming tame and wearisome to the masses.

As sad at heart, we gazed on this wonderful exhibition of a nation's folly and sin, we marked the rapid gathering of a black and threatening cloud overhead. Now it began to shoot forth its lurid, angry lightnings, while the rain descended in perfect torrents. Great was the confusion and chagrin that at once ensued. The priests and their attendants, seizing their precious but impotent deities, fled in the utmost disorder to the nearest places of shelter. The glittering, showy trappings, which before had such charms to the Eastern eye, already hung drenched, ungraceful, and disfigured all around, presenting a pitiable, if not a ludicrous, spectacle. We thought on that text: 'He that sitteth in the heavens shall laugh: the Lord shall have them in derision.' (Psalm ii. 4.) We drove rapidly away to the quiet of the sanctuary, there to humble ourselves before the Most High, and to plead for those who feel not the need of His mercy.

Such as have always dwelt in a Christian land, cannot fully realise the effects of a scene like that we have just attempted to describe. It almost paralyzes the heart and tongue of the ardent and devoted missionary. What can his feeble voice do to arrest the progress of these infatuated idolaters? How unheeded falls the story of the Cross upon such deaf and unwilling ears! Yes, this is the human side; and were that his only help, he would at once give up in despair. But the Missionary stands strong in a strength not his own. He is there at the command of a Saviour, who 'is able to save even to the uttermost,' and who left no sinner out of His wondrous plan of salvation. So when his heart is overwhelmed, the messenger of mercy stays himself upon the sure word of promise: 'The gods that have not made the heavens and the earth, even they shall perish from the earth, and from under these heavens.' (Jeremiah x. 11.) 'And the kingdom and dominion, and the greatness of the kingdom under the whole heaven, shall be given to the people of the saints of the Most High, whose kingdom is an everlasting kingdom, and all dominions shall serve and obey Him.' (Daniel vii. 27.)

At the end of the Mission grounds stood the native printing-press. There, God's precious Word was just then being printed, in the beautiful, improved Canarese type, which owes so much to the united labours of Rev. T. Hodson and Rev. D. Sanderson. Beside the printing-press was the handsome Anglo-Vernacular Institution, one of the finest buildings at that time in Bangalore. Of this, my husband had been Principal for nearly four years; and it was one of my greatest pleasures to visit it occasionally. Before landing in India, I was prepared to find the Hindu race very bright and intelligent. Yet it was with mingled admiration and surprise that I listened to the students of the first class, as they went over the evidences of Christianity with a readiness which would put to shame many educated youths, I fear, in our own land. The ease and rapidity, too, with which they would fill the blackboard with a difficult problem in algebra, was not less remarkable.

Who has not heard of the caste of India? In no other land does this mighty barrier to all national progress exist. The Hindus believe it to be of Divine origin, and they are separated by it into four great divisions. Far above the others stand the proud and dignified Brahmans, strong in their uncontested rights from time immemorial. Sprung as the *shastras* declare, from the mouth of Brahma the creator, they claim to possess a monopoly of all goodness. They are the priests and teachers of the people, and the various inferior castes must honour them, and freely offer gifts to them on every festive occasion. Just below the Brahmans come the Kshetriyas, or military caste; next the Vaisyas, or merchant caste; and last, the Shudras, or labouring classes. The members of the different castes can neither enter each other's houses, eat together, nor intermarry. A Brahman may not even touch the clothes of a low caste man without defilement. But beneath and outside the sacred line altogether, comes a class abhorred and shunned by all his countrymen, and everywhere regarded by them as the dregs of humanity. Their very presence is pollution. This is the poor, degraded pariah, or outcast. To be put out of caste is esteemed the last of all evils by a Hindu.

By far the greater number of the students in our Institution were Brahmans, but within its walls all such distinctions were unknown. Here, if never before or again, the down-trodden pariah stood on equal ground with the wealthy Brahman. They studied side by side, and enjoyed the same rights and privileges. The students understood this, and seldom indeed did they offer any opposition to this rule. On one occasion two high-caste youths were competing for the first place in their class. Just as they were nearly equal, a relative of one of them died. When the last rites were performed, the young man returned as usual to school, though ceremonially unclean. His rival indignantly protested against this unheard of innovation. But the Brahman smiled, and quietly remarked, '*There is no caste in the Mission Institution.*'

The Missionary watched the progress of all the pupils in the various classes with great interest, but on the lads who had climbed up step by step to his own class, he bestowed a wealth of love. I soon found that to know them was to love them too; and oh, how our hearts coveted these noble looking young men for the Lord Jesus!

One of these native gentlemen rises before me now, just as he so often used to stand, erect and tall, leaning with one arm on the top of the study table, gazing into the face of his beloved teacher. How often did the large tear-drop gather in his soft, dark eye, as they talked together on the duty of confessing Christ! Athasheshalu was, by birth, a high-caste Brahman; though being a Tamulian, his complexion was darker than that of many of his Canarese class-mates. His crimson and gold turban, long white tunic, and snowy muslin scarf falling gracefully over the shoulder, set off to advantage his well-formed, manly figure. When Athasheshalu first entered the Institution, some years before, he was by no means a general favourite. Proud, selfish, and exceedingly superstitious, he appeared to be a most unamiable lad. But as he gradually advanced to the first class, he became thoughtful, regular in his attendance, and he manifested an increasing love for study. The first hour of every morning was given to Bible instruction; and the youth had not been long under my husband's care, when he rejoiced to notice the marked earnestness with which Athasheshalu listened to these saving truths. His mind was now fully awake, he thirsted for knowledge, and he began to throw aside the fetters with which superstition had formerly bound him. The heathen festivals, which he was wont to observe so faithfully, no longer attracted him; and he ceased to perform the various ceremonies connected with the morning worship of their household gods.

His father, a bigoted and proud idolater, marked the gradual change in his son with a jealous eye. He stormed and remonstrated, but to no purpose. The young man continued to escape away to a distant garden, at sunrise, there to study and to meditate without molestation. The rage of the old man now knew no bounds. He beat and abused his son, and at length thrust him out of doors.

Poor Athasheshalu, for a time, struggled bravely and in silence to continue his studies, though his only sustenance was now one meal of rice a day, which he was compelled to receive in charity at a Brahman *choultry*. But his strength soon gave way under this semi-starvation. He felt quite unable to grapple longer with the difficult subjects which he so longed to master. In sore distress he went one day to his trusted teacher and friend, telling him that the parting time had come, as he must now take a situation at once. Greatly moved by the tale of the young man's noble endurance, my husband gladly offered him a small private scholarship, which was just sufficient to supply his wants. It was about this time that I first came to know Athasheshalu. Again and again he declared his belief that there was salvation in no other name save that of Jesus; but he shrank from being the first to take up the heavy cross of confessing Christ publicly among his people.

The long-continued pressure of overwork, at length compelled Mr. Hutcheon to resign his interesting duties in connection with the English Institution, and in the beginning of 1861 he was appointed to take charge of the Mysore Circuit. Never can I forget the parting scene between the Missionary and his own class. They gathered round him for a time in silence. Tears stood in many a dark eye, but words could not at first be spoken. Then Athasheshalu came forward, and with irrepressible emotion exclaimed, as he grasped his teacher's hand, 'O Sir! we are losing our one friend!' 'Nay, Athasheshalu; you have a better and an abiding

Friend in the Lord Jesus, to whose care I commend you all,' with a full heart he responded.

We had been but a short time in our new station, when we received a painfully interesting letter from one of the students, informing us that his beloved companion, Athasheshalu, was dead. He had been received again into his father's house, but no threats or persuasions could induce him to worship idols as before. The old man's fury burst forth afresh, and he beat and persecuted his noble son till his health altogether gave way. Burning with fever, away in a little inner room, the poor youth suffered alone, with little care and less sympathy; and his constitution, already enfeebled by privation and ill treatment, soon succumbed to the disease. All intercourse between him and his school friends was strictly forbidden by his unfeeling and mortified father. Yet they came to know that their companion died praying to the Lord Jesus, and that his precious English Bible lay under his dying pillow. Athasheshalu cannot be ranked among Christ's noble confessors; but may we not hope to find him acknowleged as one of the *secret* disciples of the great Master in the day of His appearing?

Memory recalls several others of these intelligent youths, who were 'almost persuaded to be Christians.' There was beautiful S——, who, like another Nicodemus, came to the Mission house under cover of night, to beg for a continued interest in the prayers of his teacher. He had just seen his heathen brother launch away into the darkness, with no ray of a blissful immortality breaking on his vision, no safe anchorage when the swellings rose high. There was bright, intelligent G——, also, who came to the Missionary weeping, because he felt that he ought to confess Christ, and yet feared the shame and reproach that would follow. And these are but types of many more.

Oh! who can estimate by mere numbers all the results of this department of Mission toil? The very rudiments of a sound English education, convince the lads of the absurdity of many of the teachings in their own *shastras*. Their faith in these being once shaken, they are led to inquire whether they be right on more vital subjects. Ere long, many of these fine young men become convinced of the sin and folly of idolatry also. One of our own students, who had reached this stage said, one day, 'Sir, we cannot worship idols now; that is impossible. For the present we are taking refuge in the Brahma Somaj, as a sort of half-way house.' Yes; and many more of the very flower of India's youth are standing there. They believe in their inmost souls that the Bible is the only safe guide to immortality, and that Jesus is the one Saviour for the whole world. But the cross is *so* heavy; can we wonder that they too often falter as they approach the decisive step?'

Let those who so lightly speak of 'lost labour' and of 'wasted money' ask themselves in the sight of God: Should *I* have dared publicly to own Christ if that confession involved, as it does to a Hindu, the loss of all things? Should *I* myself have had courage to take up the cross which certainly brings to them shame, contempt, and, it may be, even death itself?

CHAPTER II.

MYSORE—THE BATTLE AND THE VICTORY OF FEMALE EDUCATION.

'IGNORANCE is woman's jewel.' 'Educate a woman, and you put a knife into the hands of a monkey.' 'Teach a girl to read and write, and you are giving milk to a serpent.'

Such were some of the favourite proverbs that met our ears on entering upon the duties of our new station, Mysore, in 1861. At that time there were no girls' schools in or near the city. Female education had made but little progress then in India. In a few great centres of European influence, such as Calcutta, Madras, and Bombay, some considerable impression had already been made. But Mysore being the native capital of the province, and the seat of a bigoted heathen court, the idea of an educated woman could not be tolerated. From H.H. the Rajah downwards, all classes regarded girls' schools as a dangerous innovation.

As early as 1838, Mrs. Hodson, and afterwards her strong and energetic Missionary sister, Mrs. Male, commenced a day and boarding school for East Indian and native children. But failure of health was common then as now, and work hopefully commenced had to be given up before any lasting impression was made. A few years later, Mrs. Hardey arrived on the field. She zealously recommenced the work, by striving to establish a school among the caste girls of the *pettah*. In these days, female education was looked upon as the accomplishment of vice, and the pupils, when examined, proved to be chiefly dancing girls. Suddenly, while it was yet noon, in the midst of many plans and hopes, God, in His mysterious providence, said to the willing worker, Rest. Thus the work scarcely begun was again relinquished.

In much conscious weakness, three years after, we anxiously surveyed this unpromising soil. Our first home in Mysore was situated at a short distance from the *pettah*. My earliest efforts were therefore directed to some neglected children close beside us. Yet it was with extreme difficulty that we at length collected seven pariah girls, whom I did my best to elevate. What wild little creatures these dark pupils looked! Clad in rags, with faces all unwashed, and tangled, uncombed hair, but with glorious shining eyes that spoke of a soul within, they were ready for all kinds of mischief and petty thefts. They would slyly steal round the compound to our wood-apple tree, and collect a nice heap of the round, ball-like fruit, to be carried off and eaten at a convenient season. My beautiful jasmine shrubs, too, were regularly stripped of their fragrant buds and blossoms, to adorn their rough little black heads, like native ladies! Yes, they were very provoking; but as the little culprits cleverly managed to steal a good share of my heart as well as my flowers and fruit, they had to be forgiven, and gradually they learnt better habits.

Our first schoolroom was in keeping with the humble group of scholars. It was a small dressing-room in our own house, and my only assistant was the timid young wife of our Christian servant Paul. Elizabeth used to be sent for, and would kindly haste to the rescue, when I came to a stand still; for I had been but nine months in India, and my slender stock of Canarese was soon exhausted. Like a school-girl I had, at first, to learn every lesson before I taught it; but I found that my husband's theory was correct, to use the little I had was the surest and shortest way to acquire more. Week by week the difficulty became less, and it was surprising how soon my little pupils and I quite understood each other.

All unaccustomed to the least mental effort or discipline, these poor children scarcely had a single idea beyond what they should eat and what they should drink. When asked: 'How many eyes have you?' they would answer, 'one,' 'three,' or 'four,' quite as often as two! When I gave them their first lesson in the Canarese alphabet, how they did grin at each other on hearing each letter called by a different name, which, with many a suppressed titter, they tried to repeat after me! Our first attempts at sewing, too, were most amusing. Many a prick did the little black hands get, and it was no small effort to remember which tiny finger-tip had to be adorned with a thimble. But the dark understandings slowly woke from their lethargy, and ere long the girls began to listen with eagerness to the short Bible stories, which I tried to tell them in the very simplest words.

At the end of six months a young Missionary sister, who had just landed in India, joined us in Mysore. We were fortunate enough to secure, at the same time, the services of an intelligent native Christian woman. So we transferred my school to the little chapel in the lower Mission compound, where it could be taught by Christians under Mrs. Sykes' eye. This set me at liberty to try what could be done among the caste girls of the *pettah*. We rented a back room in the Market Street, and engaged a Brahman teacher, and also a *peon* to collect the children; for no respectable native family will allow their daughters to go out alone. We succeeded in making a beginning, when the teacher proved so unsuitable, that we had to dismiss him at once. He then did everything he possibly could to injure the newly-formed school, by going from house to house along that neighbourhood, circulating false and wicked reports. A few pretty little girls, however, refused to leave us; and they were learning so much more rapidly than our first dull pariah scholars, that I felt quite encouraged. But a bitter disappointment was in store for us. A native gentleman, who had become much attached to my husband, came to him, and asked if we knew that most of our nice, sprightly pupils were being educated for dancing girls!

India has many cruel customs, but one of the saddest is that of parents deliberately dedicating some of their brightest and prettiest young daughters for temple service. This, alas! is of a very different kind from that to which the devout and gentle Hannah lent her little prophet. These hapless ones are only taught to read, that they may become proficient in learning the abominable and immoral songs contained in their own books. While by their gestures and dances the poor girls gratify the eyes of licentious throngs at the public festivals, they at the same time delight their ears by chanting these vile odes in the presence of their gods. Need we wonder, then, that the very name of female education was an offence in virtuous families? That the dear little ones in whom we felt so deeply interested were doomed to a fate worse than death, we were most unwilling to believe. The master had studiously concealed the fact from us, and persistently denied all knowledge of it. Even after our suspicions were fully aroused, he so artfully connived with the parents and friends of the children to mislead us, that we could not discover, with any certainty, who were, and who were not, dedicated to temple service. Sad at heart, our only alternative was to dismiss all the dear little girls, whom our utmost endeavours were powerless to save. Under such unfavourable circumstances, we deemed it wiser to begin afresh, with greater precautions than before, in another part of the city altogether.

Short as her stay in a heathen land had been, Mrs. Sykes, like her lamented predecessor, Mrs. Hardey, already slept in death. Young, hopeful, and apparently the most vigorous of all the Mission band, cholera, that swift-winged messenger, bore her away in a few short hours from our midst. So while we looked about for a suitable place in the *pettah* in which to make a new start, I again took charge of my first school. We insisted on the regular attendance now of the few Christian children in Mysore. A number of nice little Roman Catholic girls also began to gather round us. Ours was the only female school in the city, so we refused none; and things were assuming quite a cheering aspect when another trial came. The husband of our assistant was leaving the station, and we were most reluctantly obliged to give her up. Only one other Christian woman in the place could read, and we persuaded her to help us. But after one day, her friends compelled her to return home.

Then I engaged one of our recent converts, a man who knew nothing about teaching, to collect the scholars and assist me as well as he could.

'Where are my girls to-day?' I asked one morning, on seeing the places of all the little Catholics empty.

'O Ma'am, the priest is very angry. He has for months been watching the progress of your school, and he has gone among all his people telling them that, if they send their daughters to you any more they shall be denied Christian burial when they die,' replied the man.

It did not end in mere words. The priest wrote off at once to Bangalore, and shortly after some nuns appeared on the scene. In a few weeks more they opened an opposition school.

We were much pleased with the attachment manifested about this time by a little heathen girl called Lingi. She used to hover about me, watching every glance, and ready to do anything she possibly could to serve us. It was the great Nunjingode festival. Her parents and all her relatives were going, and they wished the child to accompany them. Lingi was an ardent and impulsive child, and the temptation was very strong. But she loved school, and she would not disappoint me, so she came as usual. As soon as the children were dismissed, Lingi, who liked the feast only less than her teacher, darted off to her home as swiftly as her feet could run. Finding that her friends had already started on their journey some hours before, she would not stay to break her fast, but at once set out after them.

Nunjingode, a famous sacred shrine, is thirteen

miles distant from Mysore; but away went the child, hungry and alone, under the scorching noonday sun, till she joined her parents there. The extreme poverty of the children was the chief drawback to the progress of this school. One scanty cloth generally comprised the entire wardrobe of many a light-hearted little girl; and when it became so ragged and dirty as to be no longer wearable at school, the child would be kept away until another could be bought. The partially awakened mind would then too often return to its old lethargy, and love for school was soon lost.

Two years more of mingled light and shade passed over us. During these I had often been prostrated by my relentless enemy, Indian fever, but the efficiency of our school was still sustained. We now resided in the lower Mission house, close to the chapel and *pettah*, so all the children daily were present at our morning family worship. Immediately the clock struck ten, a large bell was rung, followed by the light patter of many naked feet in the verandah. Then the scholars and servants all sat down on the clean, nice bamboo mat, and any of our native Christians who happened to be passing about the time were sure to join us also, till we had quite an interesting gathering. We first sang a Canarese hymn, in which all united heartily, and the Missionary generally questioned the girls, and explained the chapter we had just read. Many of the heathen children in this way became so interested, that they regularly attended our Canarese service in the chapel every Sabbath morning.

As yet we had found no opening whatever for a girls' school in the inhospitable *pettah*. During these two long years we had searched in vain for a suitable place. Almost incredible difficulties met us at every step. Had we wanted more schools for boys we should have found rooms in abundance. But no sooner did the owner know for what purpose the house was required, than he positively refused to let us have it on any terms. The people were evidently resolved that so long as they could prevent it, female education should find no footing among them. We were equally resolute, for we had God on our side. Assured of success in the end, we never for a moment thought of giving up the effort, so we looked about and prayed on.

At length Providence smiled upon us, and made our way plain. We had opened a small depository in the Market Street for the sale of Bibles, tracts, and school books. Just over this was a nice, upper room, with a side entrance, and to our great joy we succeeded in renting it. The furnishing of our new school premises was neither elaborate nor costly. We needed only one small wooden bench, a large box in which to lock slates and books when lessons were done, and a few clean bamboo mats for the children to sit upon. In one corner we spread a quantity of fine sand, in which the little ones learn to form the letters with the finger or a small bit of cane. Round the walls we hung alphabet and picture cards, as well as a map of the world and of Hindustan. Then we were ready to begin work at once.

On a lovely July morning in 1864, after earnest prayer for its success, we opened our new school with *one* scholar, a respectable caste girl, named Lakshmi. Thank God! it is still in active operation. Though from such a small beginning, that was the parent of the prosperous girls' schools which have taken root and are now flourishing in the city of Mysore. The fathers and mothers in the neighbourhood were very unwilling and slow to send their daughters. But securing a good Brahman teacher and *peon* to entreat them to come, we wearied them by our loving importunity, and one after another was induced to attend.

Taking with me a tempting bunch of plantains—of which children in India are very fond—I gave our new pupils their first religious lesson. Holding the fruit up in my hand, I asked, 'Who made these?' '*Dhorisani*' (the lady), said one; 'The bazaar man,' exclaimed another; and one tall girl named her idol. I told them that they were all wrong, for neither the idol, the bazaar man, nor I could make a single plantain, nor could we cause it to grow. Then pointing to the blue sky, I told them of the one great and good God who made us, and who, because He loves to make us happy, gives to us the delicious fruit and beautiful flowers. That was the first of many happy talks we had together. It was all wonderful and new to them. They listened well, but, like our poorer scholars, the dear girls had never been taught to think. Even the simplest truths had at first to be repeated over and over again before they could fully grasp them.

You would have smiled, young reader, had you been present at our first singing lesson. What the various discordant sounds most resembled I shall not venture to say. Their teacher, I know, had hard work to retain her gravity. But practice and perseverance overcame that difficulty, as well as many a more serious one. The 'Happy Land,' which in the days of my girlhood we loved to sing, has been very sweetly translated into Canarese. This was our favourite, and the children soon learnt it perfectly, with many others.

The end of 1864 found us with twenty-three girls in the compound school, and fifteen in the *pettah*. Our trials and difficulties were by no means ended yet. Constantly recurring feast days and fast days, weddings or sickness in the families and family connections, which in India seem endless, greatly interfered with our progress at first. Then the woman who collected the girls became so careless that we had to employ another instead. As on a former occasion, a teacher, when dismissed, had done all he could to injure us, so this *peon* in every way tried to keep the children back, and to make the school unpopular. But we rose above this also.

One morning, while teaching the higher class, a heathen mother came in leading her little daughter, who was very sick, by the hand. Making a low salaam, she said, '*Dhori-sani* must show me favour by curing my child.' I knew that the case was beyond my skill or the simple medicines we could give, so I begged her to take the little girl at once to the dispensary, where she would be properly treated. As she seemed quite alarmed at the idea of going there, I promised to give her a note to the kind English doctor, who was a personal friend. But in a few days the master told me that the mother had taken the child to an astrologer instead, who had tied a charm round her wrist. This he assured her would be much more efficacious than any medicine. We pitied the ignorance and superstition of the poor woman, yet the incident encouraged us. It was one evidence that our love to their children had already begun to win the confidence of the parents.

In addition to the care of two schools and a Bible-class, a serious anxiety of another kind now pressed heavily upon me. District Meeting could allow but a trifling grant towards meeting the necessary expenses, and for all the rest we were personally responsible. I mention this, not to plead my own cause, but for the sake of others still toiling on that distant and depressing field. I feel sure that the dear Christian ladies of our native land who have time or means at their disposal, would never willingly lay this unnecessary burden on the Missionary's wife. With little encouragement, and no reward save the smile of Jesus, she is striving in an uncongenial clime to raise the downtrodden heathen women around her. It is enough that she has to grapple with a difficult foreign language, and give what she can of her time and strength to the people, without the harassing care of providing funds also. We rejoice to know that a new era has already dawned upon female education in India; in most cases government grants for half the necessary expenditure have been secured. But our duty and responsibility are by no means lessened. The remaining half has still to be found, and God has just committed to our trust a solemn charge. Hundreds of destitute orphans, whose sunken features and skeleton forms plead for them as no words could do, have been admitted to our boarding-schools through the terrible famine that has lately wasted the land. These must be supported for years to come, and wide doors are opening and inviting us to extend our labours on every side. 'If thou sayest, Behold, we knew it not; doth not He that pondereth the heart consider it? and He that keepeth thy soul, doth not He know it? and shall not He render to every man according to his works?' (Proverbs xxiv. 12.) Oh how much real mission work might be done by our sisters and daughters at home did they but lay this cause to heart! Will not they insure for themselves a share in the triumph at the end of the day, by at once linking themselves in some way or other with this glorious cause?

As from the Lord Himself, in our time of need we unexpectedly received two boxes of fancy articles from England. The sale of these realised £22, besides leaving a supply of beautiful prizes for our first public examination day, and we went forward with renewed strength. Soon after this, one morning we assembled the children of both schools in the verandah of the Mission house. After singing and asking them questions on various simple subjects, the rewards were temptingly displayed.

Of all the prizes, the pretty English dolls were by far the most coveted. Oh what longing glances were cast at them! Holding up a beauty, I asked, 'What is this?'

'Bombigarlu,' they answered; which might either mean idols or dolls.

'Must we worship them?'

'Yes, yes; we must,' exclaimed our *pettah* girls with glistening eyes, quite forgetting themselves in their excitement; but, 'No, no; we must not,' as loudly answered the scholars of our older school.

Promising rewards at Midsummer to the most regular and deserving pupils, the Missionary prayed, and we separated much cheered and encouraged.

Another sister had, ere this, joined our little mission band in Mysore. When she had mastered the first difficulties of the Canarese language, dear Mrs. Cummings entered heartily into the work, and, with some trials and fluctuations, but steady progress on the whole, we laboured together till the end of 1866. My husband had now been in India nearly eleven years, and failing health necessitated an immediate change to our native land. During our absence, the girls' schools were well sustained by Mrs. Cummings, till Mr. Cummings also became ill, and they were compelled to return home. They were then cared for by Mrs. Greenwood, a gentle and devoted missionary sister, who has since joined many kindred spirits in the realms of light.

We resumed our beloved work in 1869. By this time, God had permitted us to reap the first fruits from our compound school. Timmi, my earliest heathen scholar there, was now a Christian. She had long been one in heart, and she had already endured persecution for Christ's sake. Seeing her unusual perseverance and intelligence, we had made her a pupil-teacher, in which capacity she did us good service. Through deep poverty and privation the noble girl had struggled silently, but with fixed purpose, to rise above the ignorance and immorality amid which her sad lot had been cast. For years her wicked and superstitious relatives had vainly striven to win Timmi back to her idols again. At length, while we were in England, they resolved to entrap her by compelling her to marry a heathen husband. Timmi at once boldly confessed her faith in the Lord Jesus, by taking upon herself the Christian name, and she was forthwith appointed as our first Bible-woman in the city of Mysore. In

D 2

that blessed work Sanjivi is still engaged. During these years of humble, patient labour, how much precious living seed has been prayerfully sown in many dark hearts and homes, which our voices could never otherwise have reached! Oh, who shall tell what, or when the reaping may be?

Before our return to India, an opening had been found for a second school in the *pettah* of Mysore. Great indeed was our joy to find both in a prosperous condition, and to recognise many well-remembered faces still among the scholars who welcomed us back.

The first class of our oldest *pettah* school was now a deeply interesting one. It consisted of some eight fine, intelligent girls, who had been with us almost from the commencement. Love to their teacher, as well as to the lessons taught, had led them to continue with us much longer than we can usually keep our senior scholars. Seldom, indeed, were they absent even on feast days. They could read and write like *munshis* and their knowledge of the Scriptures was truly encouraging. It was to them I devoted most of my time, while the master was engaged with the younger children. On entering, they would gather round me, with bright, happy faces, and I used to say, 'Now, you shall choose our first lesson.' Almost without a single exception, the dear girls were sure to select one from the Old or New Testament. Their dark eyes sparkled with interest, as they listened to these glorious truths familiarly explained, and often did they affirm that 'there is one God, and one Mediator between God and men, the Man Christ Jesus.' (1 Timothy ii. 5.)

Four days every week we had a sewing class in the verandah of the Mission house. Margaret, the graceful and pious young wife of one of our theological students, kindly assisted me in this. Her father was a converted Brahman, and Margaret was a very superior, intelligent, and gentle creature. Her influence and example among our native Christian women were invaluable. Alas! like so many others, her constitution was soon undermined by the insidious fever which infests Mysore. She gradually faded, and early passed from those who loved her, into the land where there are no sunsets and no disappointed hopes. While busy with their needle and crochet work, the girls used to sing hymns at short intervals, and to us all, that hour always went rapidly and pleasantly away.

In the end of 1870, the oldest scholar in the Market Street school was married, and went to reside with her husband. When about to part, never in all probability to meet again, she assured me that she believed only in the one true God, and daily prayed to Him through Jesus Christ. Among these dear girls there was another in whom we felt a special interest. She was the only child of her mother, and she was a widow. On her return home from school, Taiaka was wont to talk so much of the truths she learnt there, that the sad, widowed heart began to love these blessed teachings. So every evening, while the mother prepared their simple meal, she made her daughter sit down beside her and read from that wonderful Book, which alone can soothe the trouble and unrest of the unsatisfied, weary spirit.

During the trying hot season of 1871, cholera, which so often hovered about Mysore, again, like a destroying angel, entered the city. Fear was on all faces, and the voice of weeping was heard in many dwellings. Two of our little scholars were carried away ere we had heard of their illness. One of these was a sweet, Christian child, nine years of age, named Deborah. Her death was most triumphant. Claiming as her own that glorious promise, 'To him that overcometh will I grant to sit with Me in My throne, even as I also overcame, and am set down with My Father in His throne' (Revelation iii. 21), the little Hindu girl passed through the swellings, to reign with Jesus.

The increasing numbers of both our *pettah* schools, now necessitated our removing them to larger and better ventilated premises. The days had been, when we should have sought in vain for such. But the bitter prejudices of the people were gradually softening down, and suitable places were found in the same neighbourhood. Many, however, were the adverse influences against which we had still to contend. The ignorance and superstition of the parents of many a bright child, were almost beyond belief. Missing one of the most promising scholars from the first class of the Mundi Street school, I was informed that she could on no account be permitted to attend again. Her father, a lazy and bigoted heathen, had suddenly deserted his wife and children, and wandered away no one knew whither. His helpless family, left quite unprovided for, might have starved, but the kindness of a relative saved them from absolute want. After three years' absence, the man had just returned, in the garb of a *sanyasi*, or religious devotee, his body covered with ashes. Gazing upon the runaway with awe and reverence, his former friends went out to meet him with clasped hands and lowly obeisance. Regarding him now as little short of a divinity, they escorted him to a temple, in which, for the future, he would mostly remain. Of course the daughter of such a saint, could no longer attend the Mission school.

'Who is this?' I asked in astonishment one day, on seeing a wild, savage looking woman crouching near my little girls. She wore a scanty, miserable, native cloth wrapped tightly round her emaciated form. Her hair fell in long, tangled cables over her shoulders. Hair like this, I venture to say, few English ladies have ever seen. Only that it hung from her head, it could not have been recognised as such, for it looked much more like dusty, knotted ropes. I was not accustomed to be over fastidious, or to keep the native women at a distance, but I confess the filthy condition of this wretched creature made me shrink back at first. I soon found that she was the mother of one of my dear young scholars! About a year before, the poor woman had been in sore trouble. The Hindu mother has no sympathising Saviour on whose bosom she can forget her sorrow, or on whose arm she can lean in her hour of distress. So in her extremity, the sufferer vowed that she would neither wash, comb, nor smooth her hair for a given time, when she would go on pilgrimage and offer it at the sacred shrine of her favourite idol. Poor creature! I pitied equally the mother and the child.

'Where are all the girls?' I inquired, in some surprise, one morning, on seeing but a small group of the younger scholars seated in the Mundi Street school. The master turned his face away and seemed unwilling to reply. I begged him to tell me the cause of the absence of so many, and at length he said: 'Madam, there is a report abroad in the *pettah* that you have given the names and addresses of your best scholars to government. They say that these are about to be seized and sent by ship to England; so none of the girls are allowed to stir from their homes.'

This really seemed so perfectly ridiculous, that I smiled, and assured him that there was no lack of ladies in England, so that government was not likely to take the trouble of exporting Hindu girls. But the teacher looked grave, and said, 'The people are very much alarmed.' He then called one of the little scholars up, and asked her whether she had not been kept at home for the same reason, till he had become personally responsible for her safety? The child replied, 'Yes,' and hid her face. It was my turn now to look disconcerted, for I could not understand this new phase of things. The rumour continued to reach us from various sources during the day, and at length we were able to solve the problem. The new government census was then being taken. In former years, there had been no girls' schools in the city of Mysore, so there were few, if any, females who could read. But now the question was for the first time introduced, 'How many of your daughters attend school? and are they able to read?' This had sufficed to create the panic, which soon died a natural death, I am happy to say.

With rare exceptions such as this, our work now became more encouraging, and our progress was steady. Girls, representing all the castes, from Brahmans downwards, were among our regular scholars. Much fostering care and watchful supervision were and are still needed, but the schools were no longer subject to the extreme fluctuations which had for years tried faith and patience so severely. The prime minister at the court of Mysore had heard of the increasing prosperity of our girls' schools in the city, and he expressed a wish to visit them with my husband. Surprised and greatly pleased by what he saw and listened to, he at once entertained the idea of establishing a select school in the palace itself. We gladly did what we could to further so important a step, and Mr. Gordon, the accomplished guardian of H.H. the young Rajah, warmly took the matter up. Without loss of time a class was begun for the young princesses, and is still going on under the charge of an English lady teacher.

Ere we left Mysore, the guardian kindly invited me to visit it, though it was kept strictly private. Much as I longed to do so, it was impossible, for I was too ill. My old enemy, Indian fever, had again attacked me in a more dangerous form than before, and it soon became evident that my life and work were likely to end speedily, if we remained longer at our beloved post. But I could not go without a last word and look at our own girls' schools. At my request the children all assembled in the fine, large Mundi Street room, and the joy of that morning made us for the time forget past trial and present weakness.

On driving up to the well-known gate, what was our surprise to find the school premises gaily and beautifully decorated, to do honour to our farewell visit. Festoons of flowers adorned the hall. The floor was nicely carpeted, coloured glass balls and lamps hung suspended from the roof, and chairs were placed for us at the farther end. A graceful arch was formed at the entrance, composed entirely of garlands and chains of flowers, arranged so as to fall to the ground at each side and rising high in the centre. The prime minister was there, waiting our arrival, with some fifty parents and 135 scholars, all dressed in their gayest cloths and jewels. My husband examined the girls on several subjects, and the company seemed quite astonished at their knowledge and intelligence. 'Why must this *dhori* and *dhori-sani* leave us?' asked one and another. 'Stay,' they said, 'and we promise to encourage you by sending our daughters more regularly than we have done.' At a given signal from the teachers, the dear little girls came forward and hung garlands around our necks, till we were fain to bend beneath the flowery weight, and held out our arms to be wreathed instead. Many trays of fruit were then piled round our feet, and kind, encouraging words were spoken. After urging the children to persevere in their studies, and, above all, prepare to meet us in the happy land of which they often sang, my husband prayed, and with tearful eyes and overflowing hearts, we parted.

This was, perhaps, the greatest *present* reward we were permitted to see in all our Mission toil. Seven years before, we had, after countless disappointments, commenced work in the *pettah* with *one* girl. Yet through prejudice and opposition of every kind the feeble plant had taken root, and is still growing, thank God, in the idolatrous city of Mysore. This was indeed the doing of the Lord. Our faith had not ventured to expect such visible results in so short a time, yet the work is but begun. It must be patiently sustained by years of self-denying labour, ere we can hope to see the highest results attained. Already another zealous and gifted young sister, Mrs. Hocken, has fallen at her post in Mysore, and it may be many tears shall yet be shed ere the ripe, golden fruit appear. But the ingathering will abundantly repay all the money, the toil, and the precious lives that have been spent in hastening the glad day. Then the sowers who have passed into the heavens and the reapers upon earth will share one common joy, as they lay the increase at the feet of Jesus, without whose help and blessing they had surely 'laboured in vain, and spent their strength for nought.'

CHAPTER III.

A TOUR IN THE REGIONS BEYOND.

IT was between eight and nine o'clock one calm, beautiful Christmas Eve, and we were on our way to Bangalore. Leaving Mysore the previous day at sunset, we had rested during the hot hours at the Mudoor travellers' bungalow, and had started for our second night's ride. How well I can remember that journey! Dreaming of no danger, we were enjoying a happy talk of other days over the sea, when our conversation was abruptly interrupted by a confused storm of curses, shouts, and screams. At the same time, our bullocks were being goaded forward with such fury, that we expected the coach to be upset every moment. Presently we came to a dead stand, and we found that we were surrounded by robbers.

We had reached a very lonely part of the road, neither town nor village was near. The moon had not yet risen, but by the clear starlight we could see five or six native men, two or three of whom were holding the heads of the bullocks. The others were beating our servant and the coach-driver with a stick, and attempting to drag them down from their seats. Despite my earnest entreaties, in an instant my husband, all unarmed, had sprung out into their midst. That was a fearful moment, so fearful, that I became perfectly calm and collected; for I fully comprehended our extreme danger. We could not tell what weapons these men

SHRAVANA BALAGOLA.

carried, and Mr. Hutcheon had not even a walking stick in his hand.

I had only time to breathe an agonising prayer to the Friend who is never far away, and always nearest when we need Him most, when my husband had seized the nearest ruffian and thrown him into the *nullah*, or ditch, by the side of the road. Another quickly followed, and a third eluded his iron grasp—for that night he seemed strong as a lion—by casting off his garment. The others fled into the thicket. Our terrified servant and coachman, who like cowards as they were stood trembling behind the conveyance, leaving their master to fight alone, now remounted, and we drove off. But scarcely had we started, when the men, reinforced by two others, again seized our conveyance, and seemed prepared for a more stubborn attack than before. Once more my husband was on the ground, and springing upon the nearest robber, quick as thought he wrenched the heavy stick from the fellow's uplifted hand. Then, with a voice and gesture before which these dastardly men quailed, he rushed into their midst, exclaiming that unless they immediately desisted, he should use the weapon he now held to some purpose. Sudden terror fell upon them all; and the ringleaders threw themselves in the dust, at the Missionary's feet, imploring his forgiveness.

Thankful indeed were we once more to resume our journey, and to leave that memorable spot far behind us. Never had we such a rapid ride before or since by bullock-coach, for neither our servant nor driver were overcome by sleep that night. Had we been attacked by men armed as professional robbers generally are, humanly speaking, we could have had no chance of escape. Even as it was, one shudders to think what might have happened, if I had been travelling alone, with only a native servant, as it is sometimes necessary to do. They continued to infest the road between Bangalore and the Nielgherries, till several of the gang were secured and brought to justice. This was our first serious Indian adventure, though it was not connected with the Mission tour now to be described. At its commencement, we again fell among thieves, and fared worse.

A journey through a caste-bound and therefore inhospitable country like India, is very different indeed from one of as many miles in a Christian land. Proceeding by short stages, so that the Word of life might be preached and circulated in each town and village through which we passed, our preparations had to be made on rather an extensive scale. Because of the extreme difficulty of procuring either shelter or provisions by the way, government has built travellers' bungalows, or rest houses, at intervals of about twelve miles, along the principal roads. These are provided with strong rattan chairs, small tables, and wooden bedsteads; while the *chunam* floors are covered with bamboo mats. Three servants are attached to each bungalow: a *maty*, to attend to the rooms; a *cutwal*, to procure, if possible, milk, eggs, and fowls, the only articles of food which Europeans can obtain in purely native towns; and a man to supply water for the bathrooms.

The Mission tour on which we were now starting was to be of many hundred miles, and we expected to be away some three or four months. As no washing could be done for several weeks, and frequent changes of linen are required in all tropical countries, our wardrobe, simple as it was, occupied an important space. Then there were the various kinds of provisions to be purchased and stowed safely away. Curry ingredients to be pounded, rice cleaned, coffee roasted and ground, biscuits baked, and a large supply of bread toasted—something like rusks, &c., &c. Next a medicine chest had to be fitted out; without which no one should think of starting on a long Indian journey. Besides these, cooking utensils, crockery, knives, forks, and spoons had to be taken, as well as blankets, pillows, and mattresses. Last, but most important of all, a very large stock of Bibles, Testaments, portions of Scripture, and tracts were carefully assorted; and a pious young colporteur accompanied us on the journey. I name these minor details, because I wish our young readers to form as forks an idea as possible of the experiences of wayfarers the land like India.

Our retinue consisted of one servant, a horsekeeper, and two bullock drivers; and we were provided with a travelling coach, a luggage cart, and a riding horse. Now we were ready, and followed by many loving salaams and pray many the success of our Mission and our personal safety, we started soon after sunrise, on the morning of July 30th, 1865.

We spent a happy and profitable Sabbath with our kind friend Mr. Groves, at Palhully. The cannon-balls which did such deadly service during the famous siege of Seringapatam, were just then being actually beaten into ploughshares at his iron factory. Resuming our journey on Monday, we soon passed the vine-wreathed houses and almost impregnable walls of the once proud capital of Hyder Ali and Tippo. A deadly fever now lingers continually in the place, rendering it dangerous for Europeans even to pass a single night there. The hand of desolation has passed over all. Crowds of paraquets are now the occupants of its royal palace. On the entrance of a visitor, they fly, screaming, in flocks, along the lofty corridors, galleries, and pillared halls—once thronged with ambitious Moslem and servile attendants. Remnants of gilding and brilliant colours, yet lingering among the rich carving of the crumbling arches, told of its former magnificence.

There was the sacred Cavery, too, flowing full and strong among its pillared alcoves and prettily sculptured shrines and bathing-places of snowy white. Behind was a fine grove of lofty cocoa-nut trees, while all around waved plantations of sugar-cane and rice fields dressed in living green. Pink clusters of the fragrant oleander fringed all the water courses, and the landscape was charming, as well as full of historic interest. Yet from Seringapatam the glory has departed.

At sunset we reached the little village of Chiracooli, and stopped at the travellers' bungalow for the night. As there were but a few inhabitants in the place, we left our luggage-cart packed in the court-yard, close to the open door of the 'go-down,' or out-house, where our people were to sleep, intending to leave very early in the morning. Towards midnight we were disturbed by the sound of distant knocking, which continued for some time. We wondered what branch of industry could keep the villagers busy so far into the night; but little did we guess the true state of things. Suddenly, between two and three o'clock, we were roused from our slumbers by a great clamour and outcry among the servants. What could it all mean? A moment after our horse-keeper knocked violently at the bungalow door, shouting, in great excitement:

'*Ayàh, ayàh,* the thieves have come; they have taken everything; the cart is empty!'

Hastily dressing, my husband ran out to see what could be done. Lanterns were at once procured, and they soon discovered two of our strong, zinc-lined boxes, dashed open by stones, lying at a short distance from the compound. All the contents had been rifled, and a few articles of clothing, with about a thousand books, lay scattered on the dewy ground. A large box of provisions lay near, quite empty; and following traces of a hasty flight, our people came to a small *tope*, or grove, where the thieves had evidently sat down to examine their booty. All that they considered worth taking they had appropriated; but heaps of linen lay scattered in confusion around. That night we can never forget. All this time I was left quite alone in the deserted bungalow, not knowing what might happen to the searchers, or who might be lurking near, waiting for plunder from within as well as from outside. Thankful indeed was I when my husband and servants at length returned, their arms filled with the linen, all damp and crushed, which I had packed so carefully only a few days before. The rest of that strange night was spent in making out a list and description of our stolen property, which at daybreak we sent to the nearest official. About 7 a.m. the *amildar* arrived in his palanquin, with a crowd of attendants. For more than four hours they examined our servants and others about the place, but none of our missing articles were ever forthcoming, nor could any trace of the robbers be found. Our loss on that occasion was about £20.

It seemed, at first, as if we must of necessity return home to replenish our stores. This, doubtless, would have pleased the great enemy of all Mission work; but if ever we defeated his design, it was now. To go back would involve the loss of much precious time, and we feared that other obstacles might prevent our starting a second time on this tour, from which we hoped so much, and upon which Mr. Hutcheon's heart had been set for years. So finding that we had sufficient changes of linen still left, we resolved to content ourselves with what native provisions we could purchase by the way till we reached Hassan, the nearest European station. Our privations were small indeed when compared with those of the great apostle, who knew well what it was to be 'in hunger and thirst, in fastings often, in cold and nakedness.' Truth, however, compels me to own that never did nice fresh bread, potatoes, and other English fare taste so deliciously as they did on our completing the first part of the journey.

We remained two days at the next stage, as the people seemed ready to listen to the message of salvation. Another brought us within reach of Shravana Balagola, the principal seat of worship for the Jainas. We were astir before dawn, and procuring a second horse, we rode across the country to this celebrated shrine. The morning was cool and shady. Now our bridle-path lay through a grove of aloes and palms; then leaving a wide, open plain, we skirted a shining lake, on whose margin a water-snake lay basking in the sun asleep, and a pretty kingfisher sat watching to secure his breakfast. We noticed with much interest the ingeniously-wrought nests of the weaver-bird, which hung suspended from the tips of the branches of many trees.

The little town of Shravana Balagola is romantically situated, and almost hidden between two hills, or rather gigantic piles of granite boulders. Both of these are covered with temples, shrines, and ornamental pillars. Long before we reached the place, we could see the colossal head and shoulders of Jinéshwara, the chief god of the Jainas, towering far above the great stone enclosure on the summit of the higher hill. The streets of the town, as well as its beautiful tank, are fringed by tall cocoa-nut trees. Granite steps descend on all sides to the water's edge, and at one end stands a handsome pillared portico, while a gateway, surmounted by a tower, adorns the other.

Leaving our servant to prepare breakfast where best he could, our first work was to visit the stupendous image, which is the great wonder of the place. Hewn out of the solid rock at the top of the mountain, Jinéshwara stands in the form of a man, seventy feet high, and twenty-five feet across the shoulders. The lower limbs are attached to the hill behind, though this is skilfully concealed. A gigantic lotus flower is his footstool, and a beautifully carved creeper winds up to his shoulders. Though at least five hundred years old, even the hair, fingers, and nails of this remarkable idol are in perfect preservation.

The ascent of the mountain was no easy task; for the smooth, rounded face of the rock was so slippery, that only naked feet accustomed to such places could find safe footing. But accepting the eagerly proffered help of two native guides, we soon found ourselves near the top, hot and panting. We next ascended several flights of granite steps, in the crevices of which small ferns grew in great variety. Passing several pillars and shrines, we came to the open temple, or granite wall, twenty feet high, by which the idol is enclosed. The space within is filled with niches containing many deities made of wood, marble, and other material. The massive gateway is cut through a giant boulder; and here we were peremptorily ordered to take off our shoes, for the ground was holy. We refused to do this, and were then more civilly informed that we might still enter by giving a handsome gratuity to cleanse their god on our departure. We politely declined this proposal also; and, finding us resolute, the men yielded and invited us to go in.

They immediately prostrated themselves before the idol; and I confess it was much less wonderful to us that they should pay homage to such an image, than to the hideous and insignificant deities at whose feet we have so often seen the Hindus bow. The priests now offered us limes and flowers, and as we had desecrated the sacred enclosure by entering without uncovering our feet or offering them a present of any kind, they had rather a clever revenge. One of them had been giving us the history of Jinéshwara rising from a cave inside the rock in a single night; and with the utmost gravity he assured us that the cavern was still there, and could be seen by any one. Pointing to a grating in front of the image, he said that was the opening to it. Wishing to know what it really was, Mr. Hutcheon stooped down to look, but of course could see nothing. No sooner, however, had he bent low to examine it, than I saw at a glance that for once my cautious husband had been cunningly caught by these wily priests; for unwittingly they had made him bow down in front of their idol! But during all the rest of that interesting day he in turn had his revenge. To crowds of the town's people and to their great *swámi*, or lord, in his own *matha,* Jesus Christ and Him crucified was exalted as 'the Way, the Truth, and the Life.'

The sun was now blazing overhead, and we had not yet breakfasted; so on descending we gladly availed ourselves of the shelter of a little verandah, which a merchant kindly offered us. We sat down to eat; but the street was immediately thronged by curious spectators. Our servant, finding remonstrance vain, hung up a horse-rug to screen us a little from so many inquisitive eyes. My husband soon went out to look through the place, followed by all the men and boys, while I remained to rest a while. A native policeman tried hard to send the women away, but he found himself unequal to the task.

'Why must we go; are we not women as well as the *dhori-sani?*' demanded one courageous old lady.

'I have a little business to do at this shop, so I am not going yet,' exclaimed another.

At this juncture they peered round the rug, and seeing me greatly amused, they became quite resolute, and the poor *peon* left us together. I was arranging some ferns that I had gathered on the rock between sheets of paper to preserve them, and the native women watched me with wondering eyes. I smiled, and told them why I loved these, and that one day I should send them across the great sea to England. They looked at each other in mute amazement to hear me speak their own language. The chief talker then asked:

'Has the *dhori-sani* been up the mountain to see the god? Does she know what great gifts he bestows upon us?'

I said I did not, when she eagerly continued: 'He gives us the blessing of children, of health, of riches, and of happiness.' I assured her that I had not gone up to obtain these, or any favour from the image there, knowing a better way to secure true riches and eternal happiness.

But just then our short interview was put a stop to by the arrival of a messenger from the *swámi*, inviting us to visit him at his *matha*, or priestly residence. Thither we at once proceeded, and at the entrance were politely asked to take off our shoes. We explained that Europeans show respect by uncovering the head instead of the feet, so we were permitted to enter. A stone verandah, supported by twelve carved pillars, enclosed a square courtyard. The inner walls were covered with gay paintings, chiefly representing Jaina mythology. The corners were surmounted by four small spires, and between each of the twelve pillars were niches richly sculptured, containing deities adorned with mock jewels. On the right were the rooms of the great *guru*, or high priest, and his disciples, of whom he had twelve or more. He is himself regarded as a most holy personage, being supposed to have renounced all the pleasures of the world.

The courtyard was quickly thronged by a crowd, which refused to leave us, go where we would, all the day; and we seated ourselves in the verandah to await the pleasure of our host. A great bell kept clanging in our ears, and we asked what it meant. 'The *swámi* is eating, and this is always rung at such times, as it is unlawful for him to be disturbed by the sound of any human voice while he dines,' they replied. Presently a door was opened just behind us, and the great man approached at almost a running pace. He was a spare, common-looking person, and wore only a scanty red scarf. This he had thrown around him in honour of his visitors, for on account of his superior sanctity, he needed almost no clothing. In his hand he held a bunch of peacock's feathers in a silver handle. With this he is supposed carefully to brush every insect from the path he treads; as to the Jaina, even more than to the Hindu, all life is sacred.

Seating himself on a chair in front of us, the *guru* drew his legs up under him, and a long conversation began. For more than an hour the Missionary had a grand opportunity of unfolding to him, to his disciples, and to the throng in the court, the blessed truths of the Christian religion. A very elegant Bible, bound in rich crimson velvet, was now produced. We knew it well, for it had rather a sad history. Three years before it had been carefully prepared as a gift to the Rajah of Mysore from our Missionaries. But how great was their disappointment when the English resident then in office positively declined the responsibility of introducing the Word of God into the heathen palace! There was no other way of presenting it, so it was given to the *swámi* of Shravana Balagola instead. To our surprise, we were courteously invited to remain at the *matha* for the night. This honour we could not avail ourselves of, and we prepared to leave, when by the *guru's* orders, a brazen door in the centre of the building was thrown open, that we might see the shrine of his god. It was a small room, the walls and roof of which were covered with plates of shining brass, richly carved. On a pedestal at the end sat the marble idol, with a lamp burning before it.

Preceded by a servant carrying young cocoa-nuts, surrounded by the *guru's* chief men, and followed closely by the persevering crowd, we returned to our verandah, after visiting some of the brass-founders' shops, for which the place is celebrated. The clang of their busy hammers resounds on every side, and can be heard outside the town. A hastily prepared luncheon of boiled rice, pepper-water, and a kind of native pudding, was brought to us from the *matha*, and afterwards the Missionary offered the true Bread and the living Water to the men, women, and children of Shravana Balagola. They followed us right outside the gate, when, mounting our horses, we rode away to the bungalow, eight miles distant.

The track of country through which our route next lay was little better than a desert. Yet in the midst of it we found a spot of painful interest. It was a village where, in all probability, the feet of the Missionary had never trodden, and the name of Jesus was altogether unknown. At the appearance of a white *dhori* in their street, the villagers fled in alarm. 'Will he seize us?' they anxiously inquired of the colporteur. When reassured by kind words and looks, they gathered timidly round, and listened to 'the old, old story,' so new to their ears. Ere long we reached Hassan, a town of some importance, being the head of the district. It has lately, we rejoice to say, been added to our list of Mission stations, and here an important famine orphanage is now established.

My husband's first sad work was to bury the wife of an East Indian overseer, who had just died of jungle fever. On visiting the bereaved family a touching picture presented itself. The poor, desolate father sat nursing a moaning infant, and three other children lay or crouched near him, shivering or burning with ague and fever. An aged grandfather tossed restlessly on a bed of pain, and altogether the state of the distressed family was heartrending. Wayfarers as we were, we could do little to soothe their sorrow beyond pointing them to the Healer of broken hearts as well as of fainting frames.

At the travellers' bungalow where we stayed, we found a soldier lying dangerously ill, also of jungle fever. He was a deserter from the army, and this being his second offence, he had a dark prospect before him should he recover. The poor fellow seemed deeply grateful for kind words, and for a few trifling comforts such as we had it in our power to offer.

As we spent several days in Hassan, the Missionary had many opportunities of preaching to Europeans and natives, as well as of conversing with all who came to us for books. Among these there was one visitor of unusual interest, one of my husband's old students, now occupying a government situation. The meeting was very affectionate, and the tidings he brought cheered us for many days. The young man told us that his father, an influential Brahman, on his death-bed called his sons around him, and said, 'It is my dying wish that you should carefully read your English

Bible. The only pure morality in the world is to be found in its pages.'

A respectable native butler came to request baptism for himself and family. He assured us that for years he had been in heart a Christian, and that he was accustomed to read the Scriptures and to pray with his wife and children.

One evening, just as the last gleams of the setting sun were falling on the noble casuarina trees around the bungalow, we went to visit a large village beyond the great tank. We were soon surrounded by nearly all the inhabitants of the place, for the presence of a 'white *dhori-sani*' never failed to secure a congregation. A good woman kindly ran for a small, flat board, which she placed on the ground, never imagining that I should find any difficulty in squatting down as they do. Thanking her, I said that I should prefer to stand. A *ryot*, or farmer, however, drew a common bandy towards us, on the pole of which I sat, while the Missionary began thus:

'I have come a long distance on purpose to tell you the one and only way to obtain true happiness. Do you want to be happy?'

'*Béku, béku!*' (We want, we want!) exclaimed many voices.

'In what does true happiness consist?'

Significant looks and whispers are exchanged, then one wise man answers for all:

'To have a full stomach and nothing to do, that is *móksha*,' or supreme happiness!

Ere we left the village, day had long faded, and the silvery moonbeams were lighting up the dark faces and mud-walled cottages around us. Our hearts were very sad as we thought on the deeper darkness brooding over the hearts of the people, whose ideas seem to rise so little above the level of the beasts that perish.

Two stages more brought us within sight of Bailoor. For some time we wound along the margin of a large tank surrounded by brilliant green paddy-fields. Then we came to a dead stand, for our road lay right through the lake. Our servant went to fathom its depth, and found that the water reached to his thigh. This was scarcely pleasant, but placing boxes and parcels of clothing on the seat of the travelling coach, we boldly entered. Our bullocks did not relish this novel highway, for after floundering about for a minute or two, they refused to move. By the help of some natives, the wheels were set in motion, when down sank one so deeply in the mud that our coach was almost upset. By dint of much effort, we emerged safely, and proceeded on through rice-fields again. Suddenly we stopped once more, for our way next lay through a small river. We got four men to assist us in fording it, and soon after were thankful indeed to draw up at the door of the Bailoor bungalow.

The servant in attendance there was a very dignified personage indeed. He could neither touch our boots nor handle a chicken, lest his caste purity should be defiled. This was the most inhospitable town we visited during the whole of our tour. It was with extreme difficulty that we could procure provisions while we remained, and the people seemed much more anxious to hear and talk about this world than the next. In the evening we went to see the fort, and just over the gateway we saw an image so vile and disgusting, that we no longer wondered at the reception offered to the Missionary.

The famous temple at Bailoor was built by a Rajah named Vishnu Verdona, about six hundred years ago. He is said to have been converted from the Jaina religion to the Hindu faith by means of a great *guru*, called Rama Anuja. The temple is dedicated to the lion-incarnation of the god Vishnu, and it has still an endowment. We could not fail to notice the fatness of the lands around it, on which these proud and insolent Brahmans thrive so well.

I spent one very lonely day at the bungalow there, being the only European for many miles, while my husband went to visit and preach in Chickmagloor. We were not sorry to resume our journey, though we sincerely pitied the apathetic and degraded heathen we were leaving behind us.

Halabede, celebrated for its wonderful temple, was our next halting-place. It is beautifully situated in an amphitheatre of hills, and a rich belt of jungle surrounds it on every side. At an earlier period this was a place of great importance. A city named Dorasamudra stood here, which was the residence of the Belalla Rajahs. These were princes of the Jaina religion, who then ruled over a large part of India. The great tank, which yet remains, is said to have once been near the centre of the town.

It was evening when we arrived, and as there is no travellers' bungalow, our servants kindled a fire by the road-side, and prepared tea for us, and rice for themselves. Then drawing our coach up under a group of cocoa-nut trees, we prepared to spend the night there. Indian coaches have this advantage, they can be so arranged as to form a seat by day, and a couch when we would woo 'tired nature's sweet restorer.' Our people wrapped themselves up like mummies in their white cloths, and threw themselves down on the grass, and an ass, on whose quarters we were evidently trespassing, came and lay alongside. The sleepless eye of Israel's Keeper watched over us that calm, starry night, and we slept in peace and safety.

In the morning, our first work was to view the magnificent temple, which we found from an inscription on its walls had been built about 1281. As a work of art, perhaps it stands unrivalled in Southern India. The basement, five feet high, is of an irregular polygon form. Above this run rows of the most exquisitely sculptured flowers, figures, and scroll-work in endless variety. So delicately chiseled is the stone drapery, that in many cases it resembles beautiful lace. Higher still are representations of both Jaina and Hindu mythology, the whole standing out in bold relief. Most of the temples we had before seen in India were almost uniform in design and shape, though varying exceedingly in size and elegance. The most imposing part of these always is the lofty pagoda, often crowned by gilded *kalashas*, or horns. But the temple of Halabede is unique both in shape and sculpture. Its extreme length is twenty-seven yards, and the interior is filled with richly-carved pillars and niches containing deities. As the place is but little frequented now, we met with none of the proud arrogance of the Bailoor Brahmans. The people were simple, and willing to listen to the story of a Saviour's love.

While proceeding on our next stage, a noble specimen of a banyan tree lured us from our conveyance to measure it, fiercely hot though the noontide sun was shining. The parent trunk at the base was sixteen yards in circumference. From its giant arms it had sent out pendants, twelve clusters in all, which had taken root, and each appeared like a great tree in itself. The whole formed one grand, leafy arbour, measuring fifty yards from one end of the foliage to the other.

We rested for a few hours in a jungle of date palms, as our servants, and our bullocks, too, were hot and weary. We soon perceived by the waving of flags and the beating of *tom-toms*, that it was a holiday in the village on the neighbouring height. The people came out dressed in their gayest attire, with music and dancing. This feast was held in honour of Mariamma, the goddess of disease, whose favour is eagerly sought by all classes. To give *éclat* to the occasion, the villagers had borrowed other two idols from the adjacent hamlets, and they were carrying them about in palanquins with great animation. The Missionary went up to meet them, and began to tell them kindly that these dumb images were no gods, and that their worship was an insult to the great God of creation and salvation. The simple people listened with wonder and interest. They laid down the palanquins containing their idols, and looked into each other's faces as if half ashamed of what they had been doing. How much more likely did these babes seem to enter the kingdom than the proud, self-righteous pharisees of the next town, Banawar, which presented a striking contrast in every respect! The sun was just setting as we entered the place, dusty and fatigued, for that stage had been unusually long.

In the days of Hyder Ali, Banawar was a large and rather important town, though it now contains only 1,500 inhabitants. The walls of a ruined palace are still to be seen within the fort. On our errand becoming known in the *pettah*, a crowd of three-marked or Vishnuite Brahmans, came to meet us, and with a look of unutterable contempt, pointed to the *pariah* end of the town. There, they said, we should find suitable people, ready to hear what we had to teach them. My husband politely thanked them, but said he preferred to remain where we were for the time being, as his message was for the learned as well as the unlearned. Several of these haughty and impudent men now did all they possibly could to prevent the crowd from hearing. They walked in and out shouting, sneering, and talking loudly to each other, and trying hard to irritate or discourage the Missionary. But he was no raw recruit. Often had he measured swords with the enemy in a greater stronghold of the prince of darkness even than Banawar, so he neither lost his temper nor left the ground till he had unburdened his full heart. As he proceeded a pantheist shouts:

'If God is a spirit, has Jesus Christ a body?'

'If He has a body, then who is He? How can He and God be one?' exclaims another.

'What blasphemy! It is not lawful to listen longer. *Shiva! Shiva!*' groans a third, turning on his heel, and walking quickly away.

'It is all false! *Rama! Rama!*' echoes his friend.

'Who is *Mary?*' asks a conceited young Mussulman, who, in common with all his people, made the circumstances of our Lord's incarnation a rock of offence.

Oh! never before did I realise so deeply the amazing difficulties of the Missionary in dealing with a Hindu audience. What wisdom, what patience, and what grace does he need! The natural apathy, which is such a prominent trait in them, chills the fervour of his glowing spirit. The arrogance and pride of position and learning in the Brahmans, with the subtilty of their questions and arguments, form an array against which only a man clad in the whole armour of God can successfully combat. Oh, why are his hands—weary, ready to drop, as they sometimes are—so little held up by believing prayer in the Churches at home?

We spent the Sabbath in this town, when the Missionary preached three times in different places. Little as it was likely, the congregation in the fort was most earnest and attentive. Some of them confessed the unsatisfactory character of their own religion, and owned that a Saviour like Jesus best met their needs and the longings of the heart.

I should weary our readers did I ask them to accompany us to all the towns and villages we visited on this long Mission tour. We shall pass over several stages, and pause now to admire the scenery around us. Our road had for some time led us through miles of rich, velvet-like green-sward, soft as an English lawn, and beautifully studded with shrubs and trees. Higher and closer they rose as we proceeded, while masses of lovely creepers twined in many cases to their lofty summits, and then fell in graceful festoons of flower and leaf almost to the ground. On our left three ranges of hills towered one above the other. The greater and most distant presented a succession of smooth, green, sunny undulations, while the nearer were wooded to the top. Thicker and more luxuriant grew the foliage, till we were surrounded by beautiful jungle. But how unlike the solemn shade and awful gloom of the Tipacardu Jungle! Here we found none of its tangled labyrinths and dim, leafy corridors. We remarked, too, the absence of the rank underwood which there engenders such deadly malaria. All around us was brightness and beauty. Suddenly we came upon an elfin nook, which charmed us out of our coach, hot and sultry though it was. Enclosed by forests on every side, a silvery lake lay mirroring on its bosom the tall reeds and long, drooping tassels of bamboo, which fringed its margin. Two monkeys were sporting on its open strand, and a group of Indian gipsies, or Brinjari women, were resting by the cool, rippling water.

These women live in the jungle, and earn their livelihood by carrying large bundles of firewood into the adjacent towns for sale. In dress and appearance they are quite unlike any of the other races we have seen in India. They seem strong and independent, while their ornaments are barbarous in kind, and in absurd profusion. They wear a sort of plaid skirt, with a printed scarf thrown over their heads and shoulders. Strings of shells, bone, and fragments of metal adorn their necks and waists. Tassels of beads and shells, several inches long, are fastened to their hair, three or four at least hanging like ringlets on each side of the face. Large rings were inserted in the noses of some, and a string of ornaments bound the forehead, in one case hanging down in small pendants all over it. Their arms, from shoulder to wrist, as well as ankles, fingers, and toes, wore heavy metal rings or bone bracelets. Nor did these satisfy their rapacious taste for finery. Some had cut a round hole in their scarves, and sewn them all over with beads and shells.

On this journey I saw for the first time the beautiful lotus plant, so celebrated in Hindu poetry, and the most sacred of India's flowers. Like fairy cups, white, pink, crimson, and mauve, those exquisite blossoms, with their delicate buds and round, bright leaves, bespangled many of the lakes by the wayside as we passed along.

It is late on a sultry afternoon when we drive up to the door of the Benkipoor bungalow, charmingly situated on the margin of the river Budra. From its home in the far-off mountains it winds in shining links away till lost amid the overhanging verdure of the jungle beyond. We had travelled two long stages that day, for cholera was raging in Turikerry, where we should have stopped, and we pressed forward to the next town. We knew that man and beast would be very weary, so we did not expect our servants and cart to reach Benkipoor for at least an hour after our arrival there. We sat down in the verandah to watch the pretty green paraquets as they flitted hither and thither among the trees. The cooing of the wild dove all around was reminding us of another land, when our people suddenly entered the yard of the bungalow.

'What, here already!' exclaimed my husband, in surprise at their unwonted activity.

'Yes; too much 'fraid, Sir; Benkipoor tiger eating plenty men, Sir.'

This explained all; and their fears were not without cause. That tiger was so famous for his exploits in this neighbourhood, that a reward of five hundred rupees had been lately offered by government for his head. Many shooting parties had gone in quest of him, but in vain. He was a cunning fellow, and would lurk closely concealed till some defenceless person or animal passed within reach, when they at once became his prey. A story was told us, that when the reward first was offered, the headman of a neighbouring village convened a meeting of the inhabitants. Just at its entrance they sat down, and were deliberating about the best method for killing or capturing this dreaded animal, in the dusk of the evening. In an instant the tiger crept stealthily from the jungle behind them, seized the principal man, and rushing into the thicket, feasted on him that night!

Two mornings after this, we received a loving welcome from our dear friend Mr. Banks, who came out several miles to welcome us to his new station, Shemoga. After resting for a few days, he, with my husband, started on an important exploring Mission tour across the country. As there were no proper roads nor rest-houses, excepting open native *choultries,* I could not accompany them, but remained with my old voyage companion, Mrs. Banks, in her home.

The experiences of the two Missionaries during the seven weeks they itinerated together would astonish some of our critics at home, who are wont to comment on the luxuriousness of Indian labourers. If they did not return covered with actual *scars,* yet their pale and haggard faces, rather than their lips, answered for them, that as good soldiers they had rejoiced to endure hardness in their Master's service. But they had a glorious campaign of it together, each preaching two and often three times daily. When we should have seen our wanderers again, I dare not venture to guess, had not both become so ill that to go forward, as they eagerly longed to do, was impossible.

FALLS OF GAIRSAPPA.

CHAPTER IV.

THE NUGGAR JUNGLES, AND FALLS OF GAIRSAPPA.

FIVE days after the return of our husbands from their trying campaign together, we are wayfarers again. This time Mr. and Mrs. Banks with their two children accompany us, and we start in high spirits, for this part of our tour promises exquisite enjoyment as well as usefulness. We are now *en route* for the celebrated Falls of Gairsappa, and most of our way lies through the lovely Nuggar Jungles.

See how the blue convolvulus twines about the hedgerows as we approach the villages. Notice, too, how these cool, gleaming little tanks are gemmed by the crimson, white, or blue lotus flowers. The man who stands almost up to the waist in water gathering the very finest of these will presently lay them on the shrine of his favourite idol, as his morning offering. The birds that flit past us on noiseless wing are strange to our eye, and their plumage is of more gorgeous dye than we are wont to see. Yet we miss the matin songs, that ring with echoed swell through our native woods.

Nature is more equal in the distribution of her favours than at first sight we are apt to suppose. The birds of gayest feather are generally destitute of the gift of song. Larger and more brilliantly painted though the many flowering trees and shrubs of India are, as compared with those in our own dear land, yet the varied and delicate perfume is wanting. The modest wild flowers which our childhood loved, and whose fragrance lingers still when childhood's days are past, they are not here. Among this wealth of radiant blossom we miss the tiny chalices that from meadow and green wood and sunny bank were wont to pour their little offering of sweetest incense into the great censer of rejoicing morn.

Our first halting place in the jungle was at the Coomsie bungalow. We remarked that all the paddy-fields there were studded with small watch-towers, consisting of a miniature platform and hut, placed on the top of long bamboo posts, which were driven firmly into the ground. The occupant ascends by a slight ladder, which he draws up after him. As evening closed in, great blazing fires were kindled on every side, and a succession of the most dismal yells during the livelong night scared sleep from our pillows. On inquiring the cause of the unwonted uproar, a native answered, '*Ayàh*, the place is infested by tigers. Neither we, our children, our cattle, nor our crops are safe a single hour.' It was the shouts and whoops of the lonely tenants of the little watch-towers, as they answered each other, in order to drive off the denizens of the forest, that had so disturbed our rest. We saw a fine young tiger that had just been caught alive, and was being conveyed in a cage to Shemoga. This rather damped Mrs. Banks' ardour and mine, as we longed to explore the beauties around us, while the Missionaries were preaching in the village. Under such circumstances, it was not difficult to conjure up a pair of glaring eyes and a dark, crouching form behind many a tangled knot of bushes, as the last slanting rays of the setting sun fell in broken gleams through the leaves. I nearly trampled on a snake concealed in a rut of the road as we hastily retraced our steps to the bungalow.

It is almost six o'clock a few mornings later. The sun has but lately risen, yet we have been astir for at least an hour and a half. We cannot sit in the travelling coach as we pass through those magnificent gardens of nature's own planting and arrangement. Come, and let us revel amid the wild luxuriance around us, while our hearts send up a hymn of adoration and love to nature's God. I do not fear exaggeration in attempting to describe the loveliness of these Nuggar Jungles, for no language of mine can do them justice. They are now to be seen in their utmost perfection, for the monsoon is just over. Mark how many of the trees here are covered with flowers, scarlet, white, and yellow. How strikingly do they contrast with their plainer but more majestic neighbours! Some of these are said to be not less than 200 feet in height, and such variety of foliage! See how these masses of gorgeous crimson, lavender, and blue creepers aspire to their very summits, and in unrestrained profusion and grace link them together by long flowery chains. Some resemble fir cones of scarlet, tipped with gold, their buds like bunches of coral berries; and how exquisite are those delicate clusters of pale-green blossoms that hang drooping by their side! A few months later, on some of these creepers will be found immense seed-pods from three to four feet in length. Each seed is said to be large enough to be hollowed out and used as a snuff-box by the natives. How curiously that crooked, gnarled, old tree is covered all over with moss and small ferns! And there are the '*Bogini maragarlu*,' or hanging palms, with their great, bead-like tassels more than a yard long. Now the forest recedes, and we look down on an open glade to the left, where a peaceful hamlet nestles among its verdant rice-fields. Tall, feathery bamboos are waving gently in the softest of breezes, and the slim areca palms, with their straight, silvery trunks and small, tufted heads, lend further variety to the picture.

At Anantapoor, the only available place of shelter we could find was an old, dilapidated bungalow, consisting of one room. The new one was only in course of erection. Lack of ventilation there was none, for the thatched roof, uncovered in many places, freely admitted both light and air. At night the gentlemen betook themselves to their travelling coaches, leaving us in occupation, but by no means in undisputed possession of the small, crazy tenement. Far into the midnight hours, a company of bats kept up a series of animated chases through the room, their shrill screeches and chirrups adding to the general excitement. The eccentric circles they from time to time described were in much too close proximity to our faces to be quite agreeable. Some rats, also, big, hearty fellows, evidently much more at home there than we felt, mounted the table, and leisurely helped themselves to the biscuits we had laid out for early breakfast the next morning. It was indeed a strange night, and the cold, damp wind of the jungle moaned and whistled through the crevices, till we were quite chilled. Right gladly did we leave our unquiet pillow, long before break of day, to press forward on our journey.

On through a few more stages, one of which is Saugur, famous for its sandal-wood carving, and now, listen! the thunders of the waterfalls sound already in our ears. As we wound slowly along the side of that mountain, with the forests above and far beneath us, we caught a charming glimpse of the river Sheravutty through the fluttering leafy curtain. Another bend of the road, and we draw up at the door of the Canara bungalow. Here we shall rest for a few days, that we may fully enjoy a sight, such as, for majesty and grandeur, we may never gaze upon in this lower world again. But how shall my pen describe those stupendous works of the Almighty? The visitors' book—quite a large volume on the bungalow table—exhausts language in attempting to convey some idea of the impressions produced by the wonderful scene on the various writers. One—the Lord Bishop of Madras, I believe—has said, 'To attempt a description of the indescribable is vain.' Yet I must tell my story as well as I can, and let the reader rest assured, that when I have finished much yet remains to be told.

Down through a deep gorge enclosed on all sides by mountains, draped to their crests with the richest jungle, winds the Sheravutty in its progress to the sea. Here its bed, which is about two hundred and fifty yards wide, consists of immense masses of rock, worn by the force of the stream into every conceivable shape. Among and around these the river hisses, rushes, gurgles, and foams. Suddenly, it plunges, in four magnificent volumes of water, over a frowning precipice into a fearful abyss, nearly a thousand feet below. The gloom of the perpendicular, overhanging sides is here and there relieved by solitary plants and shrubs, which nestle in the dark cliffs.

Accompanied by a native guide, we lost no time in viewing those matchless falls from the different stand-points. First 'Silver's Platform' was visited, from which only two are visible. We next proceeded to gaze upon them from the 'Rajah's Rock.' Laying ourselves at full length upon its smooth face, we gradually approached the edge, and looked over the projecting ledge. At first, the head becomes giddy, and the heart grows faint, as the eye measures the immense distance to the yawning depths beneath. The sight became more sublimely grand at each successive visit, for we were better able then calmly to survey the whole. As the finest view can be obtained from 'Watkin's Platform,' on the opposite side of the river, we started very early one afternoon, to cross over by the rocks. The wider chasms between these are spanned by rude bridges, composed of the trunks of trees tied together. We did not feel quite comfortable as we listened to the roar of the torrent beneath our feet, or cast a glance at its rushing, boiling waters. But we gained the other shore without difficulty.

The day was excessively hot, and we gladly entered the shade of the jungle. Spices of different kinds were growing wild all around, and never had we seen foliage so varied and so exquisitely tinted before. From deep olive, it paled down to the lightest pea-green, and from a dark claret to a delicate pink. Here we saw an unusually fine monkey, very large and powerful, with a white face and thick black ruff round it. Rather an unlooked for trouble now met us. The sunbeams cannot penetrate the thick, leafy canopy overhead, and consequently the path is muddy and infested by leeches! Each of us contributed something towards feasting these bloodthirsty tormentors, but I was evidently a special favourite, for one rolled helplessly off my neck, as if quite intoxicated. Our guides, however, were prepared for this emergency, and applied *chunam* to arrest the bleeding of the wound. This they told us they always carried about with them on purpose.

We had now gained the desired standpoint, from which the scene burst upon us in its fullest magnificence. The first and nearest of the four falls is '*La Dame Blanche.*' Descending gently along a sloping ledge, it glides with easy grace, in airy folds, like floating drapery when stirred by the passing breeze, into the depths below. By its side '*The Rocket*' hurries through a narrow aperture above, and plunges in snowy vapour, from which a thousand tiny jets of foam shoot out into the sullen pool, behind a gigantic ledge of rock. Next '*The Roarer,*' through a slanting gorge, comes thundering down, till just below its cup, which is three hundred and fifteen feet from the top, it leaps precipitously into, and loses itself in, the last of the four, '*The Rajah's Fall.*' This, which is also called the '*Grand Fall,*' clears the precipice at one bound, and descends in a majestic volume of water, till the eye can hardly follow it, into the depths, eight hundred and twenty-nine feet below. As this cascade does not strike the rock, it is not dispersed and broken into light spray like the others. It appeared like great fluted pillars of crystal, from and around which myriads of sparkling drops fall incessantly, like a shower of brilliants. Behind this there yawns a dark, retreating cavern. Hundreds of rock pigeons, whose nests are in the cliffs, joyously disport themselves through the dread abyss, appearing from above, as they fearlessly skim the spray, but as a cloud of insects. And we felt little, too, oh how little! amid such stupendous heights and depths. Well might our hearts throb, as they did, when looking up from things created to the Creator, we remembered that

> 'He calls a worm His friend,
> He calls Himself *my* God.'

In the afternoon, when the sun in his westward course shines full on the waters, an ever changing succession of the most brilliant rainbows are formed on the spray. Now it spans the four falls, from '*La Dame Blanche*' to '*The Rajah*,' with one magnificent arch; and as the sun sinks lower on the horizon, the rainbow gradually changes its position, till it appears like a fall of living light.

We were not satisfied till we had descended to the very bottom of the abyss, a feat not many ladies have attempted. But we knew that our friend Mrs. Sanderson had done it, so we accomplished it too, and the glorious view from beneath seemed to banish all thoughts of fatigue and aching limbs, for the time being at least. The spray ascends in clouds, like steam from a huge boiling caldron, and the Missionaries, who insisted on going as near as possible to the falls, did so at the expense of a thorough drenching. But amid a wealth of loveliness in that and other lands, on which our eye has been privileged to gaze since then, that scene and that day will ever occupy the first place among sunny memories.

Once, in the loneliness of mid ocean, a dense misty curtain suddenly rolled away, and the regal Peak of Teneriffe loomed up on our delighted vision, piercing the very clouds. So near were we, though it had been quite concealed from us, till we passed right in front, that we could plainly discern the houses, trees, and inhabitants of the island, without the aid of a telescope. Yet grand as that sight was, it has not left an impression so vivid or so lasting as did the magnificent Falls of Gairsappa.

The next morning, from the summit of a mountain we looked down on the blue waves of the Indian Ocean, breaking on the yellow sands some thirty miles distant. Once again ere we left this region of beauty we visited the falls by torch and moon-light. The dark woods and mountains were all around us, and Luna's silvery beams shone full on the restless, gleaming waters, whose deeper anthem mingled with our voices as we sang the doxology and regretfully said adieu to Gairsappa.

We had not proceeded far on our homeward journey when we were strikingly reminded that 'there is but a step between us and death.' At the first stage, our coach had to be drawn by *coolies*, and at the second, *Eràvutty*, the villagers could or would only supply one pair of bullocks. These we gave to Mrs. Banks and her children, and we were obliged to accept buffaloes for our coach. Very wild and untrained animals indeed they looked, but we had no other alternative but to try them. Long strings of bark were tied to the outer horn of each, and these were held by two men, who ran alongside to guide them. On coming to a very steep declivity, the buffaloes became restive, and began to gallop down at full speed. First we saw one man let go his rope, then the other; and in another instant the driver fell or leaped from his seat, leaving the terrified animals, now mad with excitement, to plunge on, neck or nought, as they pleased.

That was one of life's testing seasons. To get out was impossible, and we felt that the next minute we might be in eternity. Hand in hand we solemnly commended our souls and bodies to Him who had been our refuge in many a trying hour, when suddenly, with a shock so violent as almost to upset us, our conveyance stood quite still. We sprang out, and found that, by a special interposition of Providence, a wheel was tightly jammed between a deep rut in the road and a fallen tree which lay across it. This had brought the buffaloes to a dead stand just as we neared a very dangerous bend in the road, with a precipice right in front of us. With throbbing and grateful hearts we thanked God for our remarkable preservation from death or harm, and found that even our coach was not broken. Assistance was soon obtained, and we were able in safety to resume our journey.

After one or two similar though less serious adventures by the way, thankful indeed were we to reach the quiet of our own dear nest, *home* still, though built in a land of strangers.

THE FALLS OF GAIRSAPPA.

SHERÀVUTTY, farewell. We leave thee now,
Veiled by the shadow of those dreamy woods,
Within thy rock-hewn temple's awful gloom
To thunder forth thy anthem, and to pay
Thy mighty tribute to creation's God.
Like some ethereal form all noiselessly,
In floating robes, transparent, stainless, white,
Dame Blanche descends, an angel messenger,
Bearing a sparkling beam of light and joy
To cheer the starless night that reigns below.
The *Rocket* by her side, majestic, hastes
On swifter pinion from the chasm's brink,
Throwing on either hand with careless grace
A thousand tiny jets of snowy spray,
That falling melt in ever-changing showers
Of airy lightness, swaying to and fro,
And spreading like the filmy gossamer
When by the wandering breezes lightly stirred.
Through a deep, rocky gorge, with thundering tone,
The *Roarer* hastes impetuous down to blend
His foaming waters with the *Rajah's* fall.
He, kinglike, spurns the rock, and proudly takes
At one gigantic bound his royal way,
Straight o'er the dizzy, frowning precipice,
Descending to the dread abyss beneath,
In fluted columns wreathed with sparkling gems.
All, all is majesty. The fearful gulf,
The hanging cliffs, the sullen pool below,
And mountains pointing heavenward, with the woods
Like waving plumes upon their purple crests.
As in his westward course the kingly sun
Moves on in regal pomp, he stoops to bind
Your peerless charms in one harmonious whole,
With grand, celestial arch of rainbow light.

Then through the portals of the glowing west
He hastes to usher day in other realms,
Awhile his robes of gold and crimson float
Across the azure depths that stretch beyond.
Then eve, calm, pensive eve, all silently,
Her raven tresses bound with stars of gold,
One silver crescent gleaming on her brow,
Assumes the sceptre, fills the vacant throne.
She bends her solemn gaze most lovingly
Upon your restless waters, as they shine
In broken radiance, and unceasing pour
Their dreamy music in the ear of night.
For ever, ever on ye urge your way
With pristine vigour 'mid surrounding change:
Though seasons rise and fall, moons wax and wane,
Grand forests fade, and like the withered leaves
Proud nations drop from off the stage of time,
Yet ye remain as trophies of *His* power,
Who reigns unchanged amid a changeful world,
From everlasting through eternal years,
The Alpha and Omega, Source of all.
Farewell, farewell, ye matchless works of Him,
Our Father God. Ye answer well the end
For which He made you. Ye have led us up
From things created to creation's Lord.
We part regretful, never more to view
Scene so sublime. Yet shall we bear away
One mighty lesson learnt as ne'er before,
How little man, but oh, how great his God!

CHAPTER V.

FIRST FRUITS GATHERED IN MYSORE.

THE city of Mysore had long been known in our Mission as a hard and unproductive field. The gilded *kalashas* of richly-endowed heathen temples bristled on every side; and the native court, with princely munificence, poured its treasures upon their altars. The most learned pundits and arrogant Brahmans clustered round the old Rajah, and were supported by him; so that it was difficult indeed to stem the tide of superstition and idolatry ever flowing forth from the palace to enthral the people.

Within a short distance of Mysore were the sacred shrines of Malecotta, Seringapatam, and Nunjingode, each attracting its thousands of pilgrims and devotees every year. The great hill Chamundi towered proudly over the city, crowned by its handsome pagoda and temple, containing Chamundéshwari, the patron goddess of the palace. Up its one thousand well-worn steps, cut out of the solid granite rock, we used to watch a rainbow-coloured stream of worshippers winding during the great public festivals. At nightfall they descended, their torches gleaming like stars along the mountain side, with weary feet, but laden with a stock of merit sufficient to last for many a day.

Earnest labourers had toiled there for years. Often did they weep as they strove to break up and prepare the fallow ground, for the showers from on high had not yet descended to soften and fertilise the furrows. Our immediate predecessors were the Revs. E. J. Hardey and J. S. Banks. Mrs. Hardey, a diligent and willing worker, had early drooped and died at her post. Her lonely and almost broken-hearted husband could not forsake it, even in his sore bereavement. Along with the Rev. T. Hodson he started on a Mission tour to Sivasamudrum. His love for the perishing heathen seemed more intense than ever, and he preached in the towns and villages through which they passed, as if he knew that the working day was far spent. Day by day for a fortnight he lifted up his noble voice, beseeching wondering crowds to come to his Saviour and the world's, for pardon and joy and rest. One evening the setting sun fell on his radiant face and tall, manly figure, as with kindling eye and out-stretched arm he pointed to Jesus once more. The next sunset found that form silent and pale, with heaven's signet, *peace*, on his marble brow, and his work finished. Cholera, in its most malignant form, was the messenger; and almost ere his friend or he had thought of parting, Edward Jonathan Hardey stood in the presence of the King he loved, and in whose service he was ready either to live or to die.

Stunned by the unexpected blow, his sorrowing companion, Mr. Hodson, selected a grave in a lovely spot near the falls of the Cavery. Here, in tears and alone, he laid his brother to rest under the shadow of the jungles all around, till at break of day the voice of the trumpet should bid the solitary sleeper rise. Mr. Hardey's faithful colleague, Mr. Banks, was thus left to labour for a time by himself in Mysore. He seemed to dwell in the constant presence of death, for the beautiful oil paintings of both Mr. and Mrs. Hardey, in their youthful prime, yet hung on the walls of the now lonely Mission house. He strove by 'labours more abundant' to relieve the tension of his heart and to rise above the depressing memories that surrounded him. In Yeeranagerry, a suburb of Mysore, he commenced a new week evening service, which grew in interest until we, who succeeded him, had the unutterable joy of gathering there a rich cluster of first fruits to wave before the Lord.

Yeeranagerry was just inside the city gate, on the road leading to Bangalore. Its inhabitants were farmers, gardeners, sepoys, and *coolies*, or carriers. Here Mr. Banks, with his new colleague, Rev. W. M. Armistead, preached every Tuesday evening in a schoolroom belonging to the Mission. It was a humble, mud-walled building, with earthen floor and rickety doors and windows. A few tiny oil lamps threw a dim, unsteady light on the dark, upturned faces around, while the Missionary stood behind a small deal table, and strove to exalt the Lord Jesus. Unadorned and unattractive though that lowly room was, yet to not a few of us on earth, as well as to some who now worship in 'the house not made with hands,' it will ever be unspeakably dear. It was the birthplace of many souls.

About the close of 1860 two young men came to the Mission house, expressing their desire to become, Christians. That was a glad hour to the Missionaries, and arrangements were made for their baptism on the next Sabbath. It came, and with throbbing hearts Mr. Banks and his colleague awaited their arrival. Alas! they came not. The cross was too heavy.

Sadly, like the rich young ruler whom Jesus loved, they turned away when they found that they must give up *all* to follow Christ. Mr. Banks was not permitted to remain to reap the fruit of his toil in Mysore. But thank God! the day is on the wing when both the sower and the reaper shall rejoice together.

Just after the drawing back of the two hopeful youths, my husband was appointed to take charge of the Mysore Circuit in January, 1861. It was further reinforced by two additional Missionaries, the Rev. H. J. Sykes and our beloved and talented native Minister, Rev. Abijah Samuel. We entered upon the duties of our new sphere of labour, deeply penetrated with a sense of the magnitude and difficulty of the work, and our own utter insufficiency for it, without special wisdom and grace from above. We resolved with our colleagues to wait upon God both privately and unitedly, until we were endowed with power from on high. The Yeeranagerry Tuesday evening meeting, meanwhile, continued to be well sustained, and often such an influence pervaded the place that our faith soon rose to grasp *present* results. A Bible-class was now also formed there for the young men. It was held on Friday evenings by Abijah; and while he met and instructed them, we all used to assemble in my husband's study to hold up his hands by prayer. One evening, as we wrestled, God came very near. We had seen the deepening and intense earnestness of several members of the Bible-class for weeks, and that night we claimed an immediate answer in Jesus' name. While we were yet praying two fine young men decided for Christ. Next day they came to the Mission house, and were carefully examined. Their answers were most satisfactory and intelligent, for they had been under Christian instruction for a considerable time; so it was arranged that they should receive baptism on the morrow.

Sabbath morning dawned, and our hearts beat high with mingled hope and fear. Would they really dare to be the first among their people to esteem 'the reproach of Christ greater riches than the treasures of' the world, or should we be doomed to the bitter disappointment Mr. Banks and Mr. Armistead had endured? No; for God was better to us than our hopes. Instead of *two* came *three* respectable, thoughtful young men, well able to act and provide for themselves. We knew that they could have but one motive in professing their faith in the Lord Jesus,—the salvation of their souls. Their *juttus*, or heathen locks—one of the last things with which a Hindu will part—were cut off. Then each witnessed a good confession, and they were baptized *Shudha*, or purity, *Shanta*, or meekness, and *Dévadatta*, God's adopted son.

The text on that memorable Sabbath morning was, 'Be thou faithful unto death, and I will give thee a crown of life.' (Revelation ii. 10.) We knew, and the dear young converts knew full well, that between them and that immortal crown there probably lay 'much tribulation;' yet every face beamed with holy joy. Our emotions I cannot describe; but when we rose to commend them to the guardian care of Israel's Keeper, in our concluding hymn, we felt that 'angels then were hovering round us,' and were right gladly joining 'our holy song.' We could not go home that morning, but remained with our brethren at the Lower Mission house beside the chapel, to rejoice together, and to present these first fruits to our gracious Lord. We claimed for them *special* grace and *special* strength, that they might now walk worthy of their high calling.

A storm of persecution, as we expected, at once broke out in Yeeranagerry. Fathers cursed their sons, and bitterly upbraided them; mothers beat their breasts, and wailed as only Eastern women do; while sisters joined with the youthful wives of two of the converts in alternately weeping and reviling them. Dévadatta, a tall, powerful young man, formerly the prize wrestler in the village, was publicly slippered by his enraged father. This is the greatest indignity that can be offered to a Hindu, and the heathen stood breathless to watch how the once fiery youth would avenge the insult on the feeble and decrepit old man. But he had already learnt of the meek and lowly Jesus. Like the Master for whose sake he was persecuted, when he suffered he threatened not, but walked quietly away. Men looked at each other, but said nothing. They were dumb with astonishment.

Every measure was now adopted to reclaim the three offenders, and to prevent their friends and neighbours from following their example. Violence was threatened and almost adopted; but 'the Lord reigneth,' and the young men remained unmoved. All Yeeranagerry was roused, and little else was talked about for a time. In their fields, streets, and verandahs men might be seen talking in groups about the strange power of this new faith, and the danger of it spreading further among them. The priests became seriously alarmed at the spirit of inquiry aroused on all hands. They summoned a great *pancháyat*, or assembly, of the principal men of the village; and they decreed that all the persons who continued to attend our services should be put out of social society. This extreme measure would, they hoped, at once crush out the evil. But 'the heathen raged, and the people imagined a vain thing.'

The next Tuesday evening, after special prayer, we went to the meeting as usual. I confess to some flutterings at my heart as we walked down the dark, narrow street of the hostile village, through a number of growling *pariah* dogs that prowled about there constantly. Very few persons had assembled in the close, hot schoolroom as compared with our former interesting gatherings there, but we felt no discouragement. On entering, this text seemed whispered in my ear: 'Thou knowest not whether shall prosper, either this or that, or whether they both shall be alike good.' (Ecclesiastes xi. 6.)

Abijah first preached very impressively on the cleansing of the leper. My husband then spoke with great solemnity on the parable of the rich fool. Just as he turned to sit down, a tall young man, who had been bending forward as if to devour every word, started to his feet, and in a voice trembling with emotion, exclaimed:

'*Ayàh, wondu màtu herlutani.*' (Sir, I have a word to say.)

'What is it, my friend?' asked the Missionary.

'*Ayàh,* I want to be baptized *now*. May I go for water?'

'But why just now? Can you not wait till Sabbath?' he was asked.

'*Ayàh,* if the words you have said be true, *I may be dead and in hell before Sabbath comes,*' earnestly and with tears replied the youth.

Such an argument, under circumstances so trying, was quite unanswerable. The character of the young man was good, and as he had long attended the religious services, it was thought right to comply with his unusual request. To stand out in such a manner as a witness for Christ, and be baptized in the midst of his own heathen friends, were abundant proofs of his sincerity. Water was brought in a tiny brass *chattie.* Every question was answered readily and with deep emotion. Then kneeling down in the presence of the awe-struck congregation, the young man received the name of Stephen, for the noble confession he had made. The heathen sat gazing as if quite spellbound. Not one attempted to interrupt the solemn service; not a whisper broke the awful stillness.

We sometimes felt as if Jesus came very near to us in India. And that night there seemed but a little step between the joy of those who praised God in His higher temple, and ours who worshipped Him, in that hallowed mud-walled room. We could scarcely tear ourselves away; and had proceeded but a few yards, when we heard the angry voice of Stephen's elder brother, a violent and passionate man. He had already heard the tidings, and was now ordering him in wrathful tones never to enter the house again. This brother owned a farm and garden, and they had lived together in very comfortable circumstances. But poor Stephen had that night to suffer shame and abuse for his Master's sake.

A few days after, he contrived to pay us a short visit. We expressed our sorrow for his sufferings, and assured him of our tenderest sympathy. But he listened to our words with evident surprise. 'What?'

said he, 'has not Jesus said "Blessed are ye, when men shall revile you, and persecute you, and shall say all manner of evil against you falsely for My sake"? Are we not "to pray for them that despitefully use us," and even to love our enemies?' Yes; we knew those golden precepts well; but never before did they convey to us such a reality and depth of meaning. Surely this young disciple was under the special teaching of the Holy Spirit.

Finding that threats, insults, and personal unkindness failed to shake the steadfastness of the converts, the heathen now adopted a more subtle mode of dealing with them. They fancied, if they could but keep the young men away from the Missionaries, and from all the means of grace, they would become discouraged, gradually forsake Christ, and return to their old faith and practices. Systematic efforts and plans were devised and put in force to secure these ends. They were watched; their clothes were hidden; they were closely followed wherever they went, while every motive of fear and of kindness was tried.

It was a well devised scheme, and for a short time the relatives succeeded in keeping the converts away. But the Spirit of God was mightily at work. The Christians felt very unhappy, and they hungered for the communion of saints. The heathen even permitted them to read the Bible and pray in their own houses, on condition that it was done silently. Anything but intercourse with their fellow disciples or their teachers, they would consent to. But prayer was heard on their behalf. The faith and courage of the young men rose high; they boldly confessed Christ, and resolutely surmounting all opposition, they soon worshipped regularly with us again.

One day, two of the Missionaries went into Yeeranagerry, to try if they could calm the excitement and alarm of the people, by kind reasoning and loving words. But the spirit manifested by the villagers was fierce and bitter in the extreme; they would listen to nothing. One very wicked old man, seizing my husband with both hands declared that he would kill his apostate son, then one of our Missionaries, and finally go and hang himself on one of the trees right in front of our door! His wife, whose face was dark as a thunder cloud, kept exclaiming, 'Though I have made salaam a hundred times, you are not away yet.'

Ah, who shall limit the power of saving grace? How shall we ever doubt that God is able to save to the *uttermost,* since we have lived to see that old blaspheming idolater, with his equally superstitious and degraded wife, sitting at the feet of Jesus, and rejoicing to be numbered among His witnesses and disciples? That aged heathen woman was indeed a wonderful trophy. With her, life's best days were past. She knew that but a little while remained in which she could glorify Christ, by showing her sincerity, and the reality of the change wrought in her, by her fruits. But she did much in a very short time. Perhaps it was because she felt she owed such a mighty debt to her Lord, that she loved Him more ardently than many. But in His praise she could not be silent. It was a simple message she had to carry into the dark homes around her, only *Jesus,* and His wonderful love. Yet thank God! that story never loses its blessed freshness. Her friends and neighbours *must* hear it; and it might be they would be lured by its sweetness, as she had been. Such was her constant mission and hope, and dark though her mind had been before, she seemed to be growing daily in knowledge and in grace, under the teaching of the Holy Spirit. But apart from her testimony, the woman was in herself a powerful sermon. Even the most ignorant heathen around her could not fail to be impressed by that changed life.

The months of that year passed away, and another fine youth, who had long been an inquirer after truth, decided for Christ. At his own request, he was baptized Shanta, the name of one of our first converts, whose character and disposition he greatly admired. His parents were sorely displeased and disappointed by his becoming a Christian, yet they were most unwilling to lose their son. He was a young man of much promise, and the chief hope of his family; so to our joy he continued to reside with them. We believed that the steady shining of his light in that heathen home would not be in vain.

But a fiery ordeal was at hand to test the faith of poor Shanta. Among the Hindus in southern India, nearly all the weddings are celebrated in the months of April, May, or June, these being considered as by far the most auspicious. Shanta's brother was then about to be married. Preparations were being made, and invitations issued; but to the intense mortification of his parents, they were coolly declined. No one would consent to take part in the festivities, so long as a Christian remained in the family circle. The men of their caste plainly told Shanta's father that he must submit to one of two things. He must persuade or compel his son to abandon Christianity at once, or altogether disown him. If he failed to comply with these terms, both he, his wife, and family should be treated as outcasts. It was a struggle, for the parents fondly loved their boy; but the cruel alternative was not to be thought of. They must not and would not give up their respectability and position among their neighbours. They now besieged poor Shanta afresh with entreaties, remonstrances, promises, and severe threats; but by God's help he wavered not.

A great *pancháyat* was called together, and the youth was summoned to stand before it. Tears, prayers, and arguments were once more tried by his parents, while a torrent of abuse and invective was hurled at him by the assembly. It was a trying hour, but Jesus stood by His young servant, giving him all needful courage and grace. He declared that he was most willing to remain with and help his father and mother in every way, as far as he possibly could, but deny Christ he could not.

'I may,' said he, 'be disowned by my parents, and be treated as an outcast by all my people; but I cannot forsake Christianity, and worship idols again.'

Then the *pancháyat* decreed that all further discussion was useless. The poor mother wailed and wept bitterly, but superstition and the fear of man overcame parental affection in the heart of his father. He stood up before the assembly, and publicly signed a document, declaring that Shanta was no longer his son, and that henceforth he considered him as dead. The Christian youth was now roughly driven from his home, with only one old cloth wrapped round him, and sternly commanded to return no more. Thanking God for such a noble testimony to the power of religion, we joyfully took the wanderer in, and gave to him shelter and protection in the Mission compound.

The very next day a similar scene was witnessed in Yeeranagerry again; in the case of Dévadatta, one of our first converts, who had already borne much persecution nobly for the sake of his Master. His father, himself a priest in the village, had made his son a *jogi*, or devotee, when a boy, and he had followed a mendicant life for ten years. On account of the conversion of the young man to Christianity, the father was not invited as formerly to the marriage festivals this year, for his son yet resided with him. Stung by the slight thus offered, the old man's wrath and indignation were now kindled afresh against Dévadatta; and he resolved to follow the example of Shanta's father.

Again the *pancháyat* was summoned; and as they conducted the Christian to it, all his friends and relatives began to weep, beat their breasts, and utter loud lamentations, as at a funeral. His parents fell at his feet, and implored him to return to the customs of his people, and renounce this new faith, which was bringing such disgrace and ruin upon them. But Dévadatta had fully counted the cost, and was prepared to follow his Saviour, even through much tribulation. Sorrowfully but calmly he looked upon them, and then, in the presence of the assembled village, he said: 'Father, mother, I am prepared to do or suffer anything, but I can never worship an idol again. I can never give up the Lord Jesus.' It was now 10 a.m., when, with his young wife and child, he was turned out of his home, without a single *anna*—a coin, the value of three halfpence. The poor girl sat down with her little boy in front of the schoolroom, and wept, for that day they had no food. In the evening, however, one of his relations was moved by the sight of their distress, and offered them a shelter within his house for a few days. Four had passed, when a hasty message was sent to Dévadatta, begging him to go at once to his father, who had been suddenly seized with alarming illness. He was the only son, the stay and support of the family; so in his sickness the old man's heart grew softer, and he invited the young Christian to return with his wife and child on his own terms.

We were much cheered soon after these events, by the baptism of another youth of uncommon sweetness and promise. He had for some time been head boy in our vernacular school at Yeeranagerry, and for two years he had been a most hopeful student in our English Institution. He diligently embraced every opportunity of listening to the truths of the Bible, and accepted them with his whole heart. He was the first scholar to be baptized from this school, and right manfully did he confess Christ, though scarcely seventeen years of age. He was named Praemakanu, or Charity, which suited well the loveliness of his disposition and character. The young disciple has ever since held on the even tenour of his way. He is now a valuable and beloved catechist, and will ere long, we trust, be a regularly ordained Minister to his people.

A ludicrous incident occurred a little later in connection with Praemakanu and Shanta, who had for some time been his fellow student. The government census was being taken, when all the scholars had to give the names of their parents. On looking over the paper, we were not a little amused to see standing opposite the names of these two young men, 'the Rev. J. Hutcheon,' as father! On being asked why they wrote this, they replied with all simplicity, 'Sir, you have been to us what no earthly father has ever been, therefore we consider you to be our father in the truest sense.'

Perhaps one other specimen of the first fruits God gave us in Mysore will suffice here. He was the earliest gathered into the heavenly garner. In our Canarese school in Yeeranagerry, among many brighter lads was one who attracted little attention. He had considerable difficulty in competing with his classmates, for he was delicate and learned slowly. His mind gradually opened to the teachings of God's Word, and he became thoughtful and serious. Our Christian young men were wont to meet for prayer in the evenings at the schoolroom, and this youth, whose brother was one of our early converts, begged to be allowed to join them.

In the beginning of 1864 a severe outbreak of cholera spread dismay throughout the village. Some sixty persons were prostrated by it in one street, and many died. The lad became exceedingly alarmed, for conscience told him that he was not prepared to meet the God in whom he now believed. He became a sincere seeker of salvation, and he often came to the Mission house for further instruction. He was baptized along with two others, receiving the name of Jivawashanu, which means, 'one who has obtained life.' We did not know then that he was so soon to realise in his happy experience the truth of his name, and that he was to be the first of all his Christian companions to enter into life. But so it was; for he died the death of the righteous about one year after his baptism. From that day to the hour when he went to be with Jesus, Jivawashanu was deeply in earnest about making his calling and election sure. He might have passed away quietly, as little noticed as he had been in life, but for the manner of his death, and the effect produced by it in Yeeranagerry.

He had been ill for several weeks, but he bore his sufferings without a murmur. He became bolder now in confessing Christ, and was often heard to pray aloud, even in the presence of his heathen parents. His elder brother, our colporteur, was away on a long Mission tour when Jivawashanu sickened; and he returned to find him just about to enter the valley of the shadow of death. The meeting was a very solemn and affecting one; for they were the only Christians in the family.

'Are you afraid to die, Jivawashanu?' inquired Shanta.

'No; I have no fear of death. All must die sooner or later, the rich as well as the poor. This is a world of trial and sorrow; but in heaven all is happiness and rest. Since God has so graciously brought me to accept of Jesus in my youth, I am willing to die.'

'Are you now abiding in Christ?'

'I *am* abiding in Christ by faith.'

'Do you believe fully that Jesus shed His precious blood for you?'

With great earnestness the dying youth replied:

'Most certainly I *do* believe that.'

A few moments before he expired Jivawashanu requested his parents to leave him for a little while. Then he said to Shanta:

'Brother, lift me up and pray for me.'

'Shall I run and call some of our Christian young men?' asked Shanta.

'There is no time,' he replied.

'Shall I read a portion of God's Word?'

Again, 'There is no time,' replied the dying youth. 'Do you kneel down and pray for me.'

In tears and sorrow Shanta did so, and Jivawashanu responded, 'Amen,' to every petition. He then exclaimed 'Brother, give me your hand.' For a moment he grasped it; then the relaxing pressure told Shanta that the lad had passed beyond the touch of pain, persecution, and sin for ever.

Early the next morning, the Missionary sent a catechist to make the necessary arrangements for a Christian funeral, promising that he would go and bury the young man as soon as all was ready. He was just returning from preaching in the *pettah* at nine a.m., when a message was sent that the parents would not give up the corpse, but were determined to have their son buried according to heathen customs. For this purpose they had already made the needful preparations. My husband immediately mounted his horse, and rode off to the village, taking two *peons*, or native policemen, with him. There were about one hundred persons collected about the door and in the lane. Finding it in vain to reason with them, he told the parents very firmly, that they need not attempt further resistance; for their son in life was a Christian, and as a Christian he must be laid in the grave. Awed by the quiet decision of his words, they at length submitted; and even listened silently while the Missionary pointed them to the Saviour on whom the dead had trusted, and the heaven where he had gone. Leaving a *peon* in charge, to prevent further disturbance, he left for a short time to breakfast, returning at noon. All was in readiness, so the Missionary read part of Matthew xxv., and then explained it to nearly fifty women, and as many men, concluding with prayer. Some of them now began to howl and beat their mouths and breasts as only Eastern mourners can do, and it required all my husband's courage and tact to calm the tumult a little. He then walked through the village before the corpse, which was carried by a band of Christian young men, and many of the heathen followed it to the graveyard.

Yeeranagerry was now in an uproar. 'The *padre* has come, and buried the lad as a Christian. Such a thing was never seen or heard of in our village since it was founded,' said some. 'We must expel every Christian from our midst, or they will bring ruin upon us all,' exclaimed others. A few, however, who knew the Missionaries better, and had often listened to their preaching, stood up to defend them now. 'Has not the *padre sahib*, with love like that of a father, come and buried the boy himself? Is not the Christian way a good one after all?'

Some sensible women, who had closely observed everything, seemed deeply impressed, and strove to comfort the disconsolate mother of Jivawashanu by saying, 'Your son has had a good death, why should you weep? None of our husbands or sons ever died so well!'

'God hath chosen the foolish things of the world to confound the wise; and God hath chosen the weak things of the world to confound the things that are mighty; and base things of the world, and things which are despised, hath God chosen, yea, and things which are not, to bring to nought things that are.' (1 Corinthians i. 27, 28.)

THE NIELGHERRY TRIBES.

CHAPTER VI.

THE BLUE MOUNTAINS.

'YOU must go home, or immediately try the effect of complete change and rest, either on the hills or at the coast.' Such was the verdict of our kind doctor, after he had tried in vain to conquer the Indian fever, which for two years had been consuming my strength and undermining my constitution. It was a great trial for me to leave my home just then, but there was really no help for it; so I chose the Nielgherries, or Blue Mountains, which were easily accessible from Mysore.

My husband could only spare sufficient time to see me safely there, and at once return to his duties. The journey by bullock transit usually occupied about two days, and we were soon ready to start. About half way, our road led us through the heart of the great Tipacardu Jungle. Oh, what a silent, awful solitude! The Nuggar Jungles were bright and beautiful, but here as we wound through the seemingly interminable forest, we felt as if we had got beyond the habitable parts of creation. All around us, strong and majestic, rose the valuable teak tree, with its dense, heavy foliage, and clusters of white blossoms. These form the pillars of this vast, leafy temple. What lofty corridors! What dim, mysterious aisles those magnificent bamboos have woven on every side! How closely do their long, graceful tendrils of softest green arch over and interlace each other! In vain that blazing sun shoots down his golden lances on the broad, leafy canopy. They gleam and flash upon the foliage, but cannot penetrate to the rank underwood below. This is the hot-bed where the most deadly malaria is engendered, especially after the monsoon. How many travellers, in quest of health, have found a grave from fever caught while passing through such jungles!

It is midnight, and we have just passed the moaning Tipacardu River, which flows through the heart of this primeval forest. The moon has risen, and throws a shower of silvery radiance on the dark, restless waters. It lights up, too, the splendid fringe of bamboo, which bends gracefully over, till the leafy points almost touch the ripples. The solemn stars, far larger and more lustrous than those which greeted the eye of our childhood, are looking down into our faces, as with strange awe we view the scene around us. We almost shudder as we remember that here the wild elephant, the tiger, and other beasts of prey which dwell there, come forth in the darkness to slake their thirst.

From the bridge just crossed, we come to a very steep ascent. Our bullocks are weary, and they utterly refuse, when about midway from the top, to breast the height. Goading and clucking, as well as dragging, are freely tried, but to no purpose, and our coach begins to slip backwards. In an instant my husband and our servant have sprung down, and catching hold of the wheels they grasp them tightly and secure them with stones. Meanwhile the *bandywálla* is despatched with all haste to the nearest stage for assistance. It was a long half-hour and more ere the sleepers could be aroused and fresh bullocks brought, but at length we were safely under way again.

Suddenly a tall, dark figure emerged from his hut on the edge of the jungle, and ran after us with pleading gestures and outstretched hand. It was a poor maniac, whose slumbers had been broken by the unusual clamour at the midnight hour. In a state of almost complete nudity, he insisted on running alongside for a considerable distance, talking to us in a low, musical, and very plaintive voice in Hindustani. Soon the dreamy forest arcades, the murmuring river, the wild beasts, and the poor maniac all faded or mingled in one confused haze, and we sank into blissful unconsciousness.

When we woke, the gloom of the jungle lay far behind, and we had commenced the ascent of the *ghaut*, or pass, drawn now by four bullocks. Gloriously bright and full, like some angel eye, the morning star was calmly keeping vigil o'er the scene of grandeur and surpassing loveliness around us. Our road wound round and round in serpentine form ever upward. On one side magnificent heights, whose summits seemed to pierce the clouds, rose precipitously, while yawning depths descended as abruptly on the other. Oh what cliffs and crags! What luxuriant vegetation clothed the rugged sides of those awful precipices! Along one, a beautiful cascade came dashing and thundering from pinnacles far above us.

At the top of the *ghaut*, the tableland presents a striking contrast to the wild, rugged mountains we had passed. It consists of a long succession of smooth, green undulations and sunny slopes. A writer has happily described it as 'a surging scene, resembling the billows of the ocean suddenly solidified and fixed while in their full career of heaving commotion.' Along these verdant slopes nestle the picturesque villas and cottages of Ootacamund. This is the largest of the Nielgherry stations, and it forms a sanitarium to which Europeans from all parts of India resort. Amid its healthful and invigorating breezes, the little pale faces from the plains lose their languor, and begin to grow plump and rosy. And the sallow, listless invalid, to whom the exertion of a walk has long been a thing unknown, soon becomes conscious of a new state of existence. Scarcely is he able to recognise himself, when in a month or two he is rambling o'er hill and dale, with life no longer a weariness, but a delight. Numbers of exquisite little woods called *sholahs*, growing out of marshy hollows, nestle in the clefts and ravines, greatly adding to the beauty of the hill-sides. There the crimson rhododendron tree is laden with the richest clusters, and a delicate white camellia flourishes in unrestrained luxuriance.

It was with a thrill of intense delight that on reaching the top of the pass, our eye first fell on the sweet flowers of other days. There they were, greeting us by the wayside, like dear, familiar faces that had long been strangers. On our glad ear, too, woke songs that we had never heard, since the day when our native land faded like a dream. Yes, there could be no doubt about it; and we welcomed the well-remembered voices of the blackbird, the thrush, and the lark again, just as fondly as we should a friend of our early years. I had once stood on these breezy heights before, when my husband was appointed as a deputation to visit the English soldiers quartered at Jackatalla. It was on that occasion, that the glories of the mountain land first broke upon me, with all the delighted surprise of a new discovery.

Our temporary home was in a tasteful little bungalow, behind and around which stretched a fine orange grove, laden with golden fruit. The morning air was filled with richest perfume, as we sallied forth to admire the beauties of nature. In this favoured region—Coonoor—I first saw the fern tree flourishing in a deep gully, and there we visited and examined with interest a tea garden and coffee plantation. We were never weary of watching the play of light and shadow on the mountains, round whose sides the clouds twisted and curled in snowy wreaths at our feet, while above all was brightness.

Oh, how varied and exquisitely lovely were the tints of the sky at sunset! One of these was so gorgeous, that, if faithfully transferred to canvas, the artist would, I fear, be reckoned guilty of exaggeration. On either side of that spot in the glowing west behind which the sun had sunk, rose two grand pyramids of dark cloud with golden edges. Between these gloomy portals was a blaze of rich, burnished gold. From this, three immense radiant shafts shot out far into the azure beyond, which was delicately pencilled over with soft, shadowy lines. Pink cloudlets were slowly sailing overhead on our left, and a lofty range of purple cloud melted into silver-grey on the right.

Once, I rode over the hills to enjoy a soldiers' love-feast with my husband. I shall never forget it. One after another they rose in quick succession, those fine, manly fellows, to tell of God's goodness. Each seemed to feel that he owed more to his Lord than did his neighbour, and he must strike a yet higher note of praise. Some told a touching tale of early waywardness, and of many wanderings from his home and his God. But in that far country the sinner had come to himself; and though on earth he might never again hear the welcome to his father's house, he had heard it from his God. There was much to tell about the joy of that meeting, and of the best robe so ungrudgingly given, the feast and the new song. And how these soldiers did sing! The interest never flagged for a moment, till the bugle call warned us away.

One morning we rode on horseback to the summit of Dodabetta, or the Great Mountain, the highest point in Southern India, eight thousand seven hundred and sixty feet above the level of the sea. And what a panorama lay beneath us. On one side Hullical Droog and Hybeck's Hill reared their lofty crests against the deep, blue sky; while in front the long range of the beautiful Annimallies, with Macourtie's Peak—the Todas' gate to heaven—melted away into cloudland. Immediately before us lay the romantic villas of Ootacamund, with its wide, shining lake and gothic church tower from among the trees pointing heavenwards. The valley of Catey, the home of the German Missionaries, Wellington, the soldiers' sanitarium, and distant Coonoor filled up the picture. Another day, from the summit of One Tree Hill we looked down some seven thousand feet on the Coimbatoor country. We viewed it through a thin, blue haze, and it was difficult to believe that these tiny eminences were really hills, these silvery threads rivers, these dark patches waving forests, with towns and villages clustering between.

Altogether that visit was one of almost unalloyed enjoyment. But now I had come to learn a very difficult lesson, one harder to grapple with even than Canarese! That lesson was to *be still* and *do nothing*, but strive to get well. Dear Mrs. Hodson was the companion of my solitude. She, like myself, had come in quest of health, a blessing that was never more to return to her. Her mature and chastened spirit, tended by example rather than precept to bridle and calm my younger and more ardent nature. In those quiet months we formed a friendship which death only has interrupted. It was her earnest wish to take her last earthly journey home by Mysore, that we might spend one week together again. But her failing strength would not permit of the extra fatigue.

Burton Cottage was the name of our lovely nest among the mountains. It was perched on the side of a wooded hill, which sloped down to the blue waters of the lake. The verandah was wreathed round by gay masses of the scarlet trumpet honeysuckle, and also by the rich pink clusters of the climbing hill-rose. Our little garden, under Mrs. Hodson's skilful supervision, glowed with the most gorgeous bloom, and the landscape before and on either side was romantic in the extreme. Lonely though our situation was, we found something ever new to admire and enjoy in the luxuriance of nature. My chamber, like Christian's at the palace 'Beautiful,' had 'its window opening toward the sun-rising;' and like him, too, 'when I awoke I arose and sang.' Then I sauntered forth to breathe the freshness and fragrance of the sweet morning air, amusing myself during these solitary rambles by forming a large collection of ferns. I was much interested too, in collecting the different Nielgherry earths, which I obtained chiefly from the cuttings or embankments. I never saw such variety elsewhere. From a rich, dark loam I found nearly every leading shade of brown, red, and yellow, down to chalk. My favourite walk was along a deep glen, where a clear, singing little fern-fringed brook went dancing gaily along. On its margin grew tall rhododendron trees, covered with beautiful bunches of crimson flowers. Some strange, gnarled, old trees were entirely covered by a drapery of long, white moss, popularly known by the name of 'Adam's Beard.' They presented quite a wintry appearance. I sometimes wonder now how I had the temerity to venture so far into these lonely places, for cheetahs were not infrequent visitors there. But the loveliness lured me on, and the songs of the happy birds made me forget fear. They came in such numbers to bathe their plumage in the limpid wave, and then raising a tuneful matin hymn, they soared joyously away.

The botany of these favoured latitudes would form an almost inexhaustible study. It embraces the productions and flora, not only of both the tropical and temperate zones, but Baron Hügel says that he 'could recognise on these heights a vegetation quite Alpine also, but enlarged and embellished by a tropical sun.' Flowers that are but shrubs at home frequently become trees here, such as the rose, the fuchsia, and others. In the beautiful grounds of Union Hotel, at Ootacamund, one heliotrope, in a closely pruned mass, measured ten feet in height by seventy in circumference. One of the gayest of the Nielgherry blossoms was the scarlet and yellow trumpet flower. Each bell or trumpet would often be about a foot in length, and the bush on which they grew would be covered with a flame-like mass of these. No hedgerows could be more charming than those of the hill-rose. The clusters frequently consisted of as many as thirty small but lovely roses of a delicate pink. I have often amused myself by counting them.

Every villa had its garden radiant with blossoms of the richest dye. Oh, how luxuriantly did the passion flower twine and droop over the trellis work and verandahs! Here too the tea and cloth of gold roses attained a size and fulness such as we have seen in no other region. It was indeed a rare treat to spend a day in the magnificent botanical gardens, which are laid out in terraces along a fine hill. Many of the natural trees and rocks are retained, and every winding walk or shady nook surprises and delights the eye with some new and unexpected beauty.

Among the fruits common in this 'delightsome land' were the orange and the apple, the pear and the plum, the peach, the nectarine, and the citron, besides the smaller fruits, such as the strawberry, raspberry, locquot, and hill-gooseberry. These were mostly inferior both in size and flavour to those growing at home, but they were much valued by visitors from the plains. And the vegetables! Why, we might have fancied ourselves in the land of the Sphinxes again, for in quantity and quality they seemed to old Indians to vie with the productions of Egypt.

Among the various hill tribes who used to visit Burton Cottage, with wild honey and other articles for sale, the Todas were the most interesting. They are the earliest known inhabitants of the Nielgherries, and claim to be lords of the soil. The other tribes acknowledge this by paying them a small annual tribute. Tall and well built, with regular features, and frank, open countenances, they display none of that cringing servility so common among the lower castes in India. Their bearing is manly and independent. The Toda women are generally nice looking, and have a ready smile to offer on meeting with any one. Their hair has this peculiarity, that it often falls in natural jetty ringlets over their necks and shoulders. That of the men is parted in the centre, and cut evenly round. It is so thick and bushy that it stands out exactly like a black turban. Neither sex wears any covering on the head. Their only garment is a sort of blanket, fastened loosely round the person like a mantle. The degenerating habit of polyandry prevails among the Todas, and at one time female infanticide is said to have been practised. Only one girl was permitted to live in each family, the others being strangled. This inhuman practice has happily been suppressed for many years.

The life and customs of this tribe, are altogether pastoral and simple. Their language is a kind of mixed Canarese dialect, and they have no written character of any description. The marriage ceremony of a Toda bride is scarcely such as would satisfy an English maiden. On the happy day she is brought to the house of her future husband, where, of course, there is feasting on an extensive scale going on. At a given time she bows herself humbly before her lord, who condescends to place first one foot and then the other on her head! He then says, 'Go, and fetch water for cooking.' The bride obeys, and her compliance with this command constitutes her mistress of the house.

The Toda *munds*, or clusters of huts, are always

prettily situated, on the greenest slopes of the hills. I used to like very much to visit them, when their fierce buffaloes were at a safe distance. These form their most prized and valuable possession, and they care to rear no other animals. The milk of the buffalo is richer than that of the cow, and consequently it yields more butter. This they clarify and form into *ghee*, which is much relished by all classes in India. Every visitor to the *munds* is greeted at once by a show of outstretched hands and a storm of, '*Elàm! elàm!*' a present, a present! As they have no caste among them, the Todas did not object to our looking into their houses as well as we could. We had to bend down on all fours, for the tiny doorway was two feet wide by two and a half high! Within all was darkness, though we could just discern a few moving figures. But the stench was such as to force me to restrain my curiosity. In shape, these primitive huts exactly resemble the tilt of a waggon. Each *mund* contains one sacred building, larger and better than the rest, and surrounded by a wall. Here the priest with his attendants reside, and all the work of a dairy is carried on within, for this the Toda regards as the most holy of all occupations.

Their religion is of the simplest kind. They salute the rising sun, and their only object of worship is said to be the sacred buffalo bell. This they look upon as representing a deity called 'Hiridra,' or the chief god. On the death of a Toda it is customary for his tribe to kill several buffaloes, that their deceased friend may be supplied with milk in 'the other district.' Macourtie's Peak is a lofty mountain pinnacle, clearly seen from their green hill-sides. It is eight thousand five hundred feet high, and here, they say, the portal-keeper of heaven resides. From this sacred height the Todas believe that the soul of the deceased, along with the spirits of the buffaloes sacrificed at his death, leap together up to *humanorr*, or 'the great country.'

My sojourn in the mountain land was now drawing to a close. Its healthful breezes had, by God's blessing, at length chased the fever from my brow, and I was already counting the days for my return to home and work again. But a trial was in store, and another lesson had first to be learnt. Tidings came that cholera had broken out with fearful and unusual severity in Mysore. In a heathen city such a visitation always causes panic; but this time it was extreme. Almost every European hastily left the place, and the people cowered in abject terror beneath the uplifted sword of the solemn angel.

Knowing that my husband needed rest, our Chairman, Mr. Hodson, kindly asked him to join me on the Nielgherries, and remain till the epidemic abated, when we could return together. It was a severe struggle; but the scale turned in favour of the poor heathen. The heart of the Missionary yearned over them, and he could not leave them in their sore distress. Might not hearts grow softer at such a time? he reasoned. Would not some, who could sneer at the offer of a Saviour when in health, now in their extremity gladly turn their despairing eye to the crucified One? I dared no longer to say *come*, and I could not go from the pure hill air into that plague-stricken city. What could we do under such trying circumstances, but just trust in Him who is 'a stronghold in the day of trouble'? Controlled by God's hand, that cloud burst at length in blessings on our heads. We had proved afresh His truth and faithfulness, and we were permitted to meet again under the happiest circumstances, and to resume our loved duties together in the city of Mysore. A new and stronger bond had been formed between the Missionary and the people, and not a few were now prepared to listen with respectful attention to the message of mercy from his lips.

THE FOREST WARBLERS.

THRICE welcome, sweet birds, as on restless wing
Ye gladden the day by the songs ye sing;
All sad were the forests, the valleys lone,
Uncheered by the mirth of your joyous tone.

A greeting ye find from the rich and poor,
At the pillared hall and the cottage door;
E'en age lends an ear, as with brightening eye
He owns the sweet power of your witchery.

'Mid sunshine and breezes the laughing child,
By the fern-fringed brook, with his posy wild,
Responds to the trill of your happy song,
As shouting he revels the flowers among.

Where giant boughs wave to the wind's low moan
In the dim arcades of the forest lone,
How soothingly falls on the raptured ear
The echoing swell of your wood notes clear!

Like sunbeams ye wander the green earth through,
The prairie, the jungle, the mountain blue;
Alike upon British and foreign shores
Your glad matin song on the breezes soars.

Entranced we have greeted your tuneful lay
At the golden dawn of the Indian day;
Though voices around us no hymn would raise,
Ye came with your tribute of grateful praise.

Man's eye on the purple and gold might rest,
But they woke no song in his voiceless breast;
On his heart's cold altar no incense burns
As the Hindu's gaze to his idol turns.

In nature's vast temple, creation's Lord
By His works is unceasingly adored:
By the silvery moon and the starry night;
By the kingly sun in his peerless might;

By mountains and vales with their robe of green;
By flow'rets that blossom, then die unseen.
The dewdrop that quivers with rainbow light
In the lily's chalice of stainless white,

The thunders of ocean, the zephyr's balm,
All unite in the universal psalm;
And the earth beneath with the heavens above
Still proclaim that their Maker's name is Love.

Shall man's never-dying, blood-ransomed race,
Alone bring no tribute, no mercy trace—
In God's image formed and for purpose high,
The heir of a kingdom beyond the sky?

Oh! shall *he* sit silent, or basely turn
From such matchless love, and such glory spurn?
Retouch, Lord, the strings of that tuneless lyre;
Its music awake, and its song inspire.

CHAPTER VII.

THE SMALLER TENANTS OF THE MISSION COMPOUND.

I SHOULD like to give our young friends a glimpse of some of the tiny occupants of the Mission grounds, for India teems with life of every kind. First among our Indian persecutors I must place the mosquito. It is a gnat, about as long as a common fly, which infests most warm countries. They are specially numerous where trees abound; but in India exemption from them can only be found in the hill regions, such as the Nielgherries.

Mysore could boast of real prize ones—great speckled fellows, known from their unusual size and strength as 'the Rajah's mosquitoes.' A more relentless, blood-thirsty persecutor than this insect can scarcely be found. Like other evil doers they love the darkness, and come forth in clouds with the first shades of evening. As night draws on, the air becomes quite vocal with their shrill buzz: and woe betide the hapless limbs that are in any way exposed to their attack. They continue to swarm around till daylight returns, and escape from them you can nowhere find but under closely drawn mosquito curtains. These completely cover the four-posted bedsteads like a net cage. They are made without any opening, and are carefully tucked under the mattress. During the day the curtains are neatly looped up; but they are always let down quite early in the afternoon. In raising a part to get under them at

SNAKE CHARMERS.

bed-time, you must be very expert, else you will certainly admit companions that will by no means add to the peacefulness of your slumbers.

Though old Indians do not escape with impunity, yet, strange to say, the mosquito has a peculiar relish for fresh English blood. Their sting in many cases produces very irritable small boils or sores. One dear old lady, after nearly thirty years of tropical life, could only obtain peace to work or read for any length of time, even during the day, by placing rags sprinkled with alcohol, upon her hands. This is said most effectually to ward off their attacks and to allay the irritation. Another lady friend found the mosquitoes so intolerable, that she had a small net room erected in her nursery. There alone she could sit and attend to her baby with any degree of comfort. But these troublers of our peace played the most serious trick of all on a young bride of our acquaintance, who had just arrived in India. On her wedding morn, to her unspeakable dismay, she found her fingers so swollen and disfigured that it was with the greatest difficulty the wedding ring could be put on.

Another tiny winged persecutor is the eye-fly. These minute tormentors appear in myriads when the mango showers are due, about April or May, towards the close of the hot season. Unlike the mosquito, these revel in the light, and dance in the sunbeams. They hover in hundreds close to and around the eyes, being attracted by the eyelashes, on which they perseveringly try to settle. They emit a poisonous secretion, causing great irritation, and frequently induce a most painful inflammation, known as country sore eye, when one unfortunately gets inside.

But while describing several of India's annoyances, I must not leave out some of her numerous insect gems. She has a wealth of large and gorgeous butterflies, and an endless variety of beautiful moths. Some of these are exquisitely pencilled over, so as exactly to resemble the most delicate plumage, of many tints, and soft as velvet. Attracted by the lights, they would enter the house, and flutter round the lamps, often singeing their pretty wings. But none, perhaps, did we admire more than the brilliant firefly. They flit about in clouds as the evening deepens into night, gleaming and sparkling like fairy golden lamps among the dark green leaves.

There were singular creatures, too, which occasionally sported about upon our walls and garments. They had very long, almost shapeless, pale yellow bodies, which at a short distance could not be distinguished from a piece of straw. Indeed, I mistook the first I saw for this. One peculiar kind of slender winged beetle seemed to have a peculiar fancy for getting about one's neck or under our thin muslin jacket. It was not agreeable to feel the insect wriggling about the shoulders, especially as its odour was exceedingly offensive.

But come now, let us watch what that fine-looking, grey-haired Brahman is so intently occupied in doing. As he passes slowly along the road, his eyes fixed on the ground, he frequently pauses, and bends down. Now he takes some pounded rice and sugar from a little bag, which he holds in his hand, and carefully sprinkles it around a number of tiny holes by the way. He believes himself to be performing a work of great merit by thus regularly feeding the ants. Our Brahman friend must pardon our lack of veneration, if

I now venture to place the *ant* next on my list of Indian scourges; and I trust our friends will believe that, in each case, I simply describe facts as we found them.

From some cause or other, during a season of excessive and protracted drought, our compound literally swarmed with ants—black, red, and white. The black were of three sizes, the largest being often nearly three-quarters of an inch long. These were very disgusting, and sometimes would sting one rather severely, and there were middle sized and small ones as well. Nothing was safe from them. They drowned in our milk; attacked any joint of meat that might be placed in the safe; mounted the sideboard, and feasted there; or forced their way by hundreds into every box or bag of sugar. We are obliged to keep a supply of such stores in India, as in solitary stations they cannot always be procured. In vain did we place the feet of sideboard and meat safe in tin or wooden saucers, filled with water or Margosa oil, which the ant is supposed greatly to dislike. They soon contained a struggling mass, and the dead bodies of the drowned ants were at once converted into rafts and bridges by their unfeeling companions. Then mounting in triumph, they were to be seen busily enjoying their coveted repast.

'Necessity is the mother of invention,' so we had a large swinging shelf slung from the roof of the store-room, the ropes of which we liberally smeared with tar, and here we found we could place certain tempting morsels in safety. At all hours, these active little creatures might be seen in armies marching in rank and file as orderly as possible, in quest of spoil. Thinking to destroy some of their favourite haunts, we had two old trees which were always black with ants cut down, yet the evil remained.

They once gained a singular and rather mortifying victory over one of our household. In order to accommodate an additional Missionary, we had fitted up a nice little bedroom just at the end of the school buildings nearest to the Mission house. It looked quite inviting with its Venetian shutters, clean, cool bamboo mat, and light, simple furniture. But, alas! a few hours' occupation dispelled the charm. This room turned out to be a perfect rendezvous of a colony of large black ants. We set to work diligently to clear them out next morning; but in the evening there they were again, apparently as numerous as ever. This certainly was annoying; but the young Missionary was not to be beaten by so insignificant an enemy. No, no; he would soon drive off or exterminate those persevering legions. So he and his servant mounted guard, and evening after evening they patiently expelled and destroyed the intruders. They filled up every chink through which they had been seen to enter, and they even used fire to keep them off. But the morning as surely found them all over the place again. Rest for the sole of his foot the Missionary found none, so after one or two uncomfortable attempts at dressing on the top of a table, he was fain to own himself completely vanquished. He had to beat a retreat, leaving the ants in possession, while we found more hospitable quarters for him.

The red ants, though less numerous, were still more objectionable from their strong and very disagreeable odour. They were so minute that they could squeeze under the covers of preserve jars, and all they touched was rendered useless. But the most to be dreaded of all this family were the white ants. They generally carry on the work of destruction unseen, and their presence is not suspected till some rafter or couch is suddenly seized with palsy and comes down with a crash. In the course of a single night they will often commit great havoc. They are not at all fastidious in their tastes, for they seem equally to enjoy devouring a carpet, a mat, a box, a couch, or a library. Fortunately, if one is constantly on the watch, the white ant gives a certain sign of its approach, and if this be observed much mischief may be prevented. They throw up a quantity of red earth before them; and the presence of this under a carpet is the signal for a general upset. These ingenious little architects erect for themselves stately edifices many feet in height, and of great hardness and solidity. Inside, these are filled with tube-like compartments, into which a snake not unfrequently intrudes. The ant-hill then becomes an object of worship, and the dangerous god within is fed with milk and *ghee* by the natives.

At certain seasons, the white ants obtain wings, and issue forth in swarms. It is a hot, sultry evening, scarcely a breath of wind stirs the leaves. Windows, doors, and ventilators are all thrown open; and we are seated around the tea-table, on which a lamp burns brightly. Suddenly the welcome patter of heavy rain-drops tells us that the monsoon is about to set in. But at the same moment, a cloud of white ants and flying beetles of various kinds enters the room, and they begin to whirl madly about our faces and around the lights. In a few seconds more the tea-table is quite strewn over with the wings of the ants, which they drop at the slightest touch, leaving their unsightly little bodies writhing and twisting about in the butter, sugar, or whatever they chance to fall into. By-and-by things are reduced to order again by removing the lamps to the farther end of the room, and placing soup plates filled with water around them. These soon contained thick, struggling masses of drowning insects.

I shall not weary our young readers by a description of other intruders feared by every one, and of which most persons have read or heard a great deal. I refer to centipedes, scorpions, and a very large, poisonous spider common in our part of India. Each of these paid us frequent visits at the Mission house, and some of our escapes from being stung by them were indeed hair-breadth ones.

But just look out now on a pleasing picture from the windows of our end rooms. That is the great hill Chamundi, which you see rising high in the background beyond the flashing tank and native gardens. Nearer, close to the foot of our compound, that little building is a devil temple. See how lazily our buffalo with her calf is stretched out on the grass under the spreading shade of that fine tamarind tree near the centre of the Mission grounds. But we have come to study natural history on this noble soap-nut tree, close to the windows, which keeps the room so cool and shady through the long, sultry hours of the Indian day. That bright-eyed little lizard hiding among the prickly leaves of the aloe yonder has its gaze fixed upon the long train of black ants that are slowly marching up the trunk of the great tree. See, it is after them now in quest of its breakfast, which it soon secures. And here comes another, more leisurely and dignified in its movements, a large, formidable looking fellow, from the thick grass beneath. How he puffs out his breast, and bristles up the comb along his spine, as if very angry. He is changing colour, too. But a minute ago he wore a greenish grey tint, now he is all aglow with the brightest yellow, scarlet, and green. Is not he a chameleon?

Those saucy crows perched on the uppermost bough of the soap-nut are keenly watching every movement of the lizards, for they are hungry too, and would not object to feast upon them, if they have the chance. But, see! there come our gay little neighbours the squirrels; half a dozen of them together, bounding, chasing, climbing so merrily, life evidently such a joy to them. Pretty creatures! we can scarcely feel angry with them, and yet they are mischievous too. They enter by the open windows and help themselves without the slightest scruple to the wool out of our handsomest Indian rugs, with which cosily to line their nests; and they persistently tear the linings of our bamboo verandah blinds into ribbons.

Our Indian crows, which I have named, were bolder and more troublesome than we ever found their English brothers to be. If any eatable were placed for a few moments on the table in the back verandah, they would pounce upon it directly, for they seemed always on the alert. Nor did they hesitate to enter the dining room when they dared, and they would bear away in triumph a large piece of butter, or any delicacy they could manage to secure. Once our servant became so exasperated by their constant thefts, that he caught and hung up the offender behind the house, as a warning to all others. The news quickly spread, and soon all the community of crows in the neighbourhood had assembled to protest in the strongest manner against the indignity offered to their sable friend. We were in the native chapel at the time, and could not imagine what the unusual uproar meant. It continued to wax louder and louder, till it quite disturbed the service. Then a messenger was sent out to ascertain the cause, and if possible put a stop to it. So the unfortunate bird was straightway cut down and put out of sight, when the rest quietly dispersed again.

A very disagreeable little animal, the musk rat, would sometimes run across the rooms, leaving such a sickening stench behind as rendered the house unpleasant for at least that day. The natives always affirmed that the appearance of these indicated the presence of a snake close by. Whether this idea were correct or not we could not determine, but very many snakes were found in the Mission compound during our stay at Mysore.

Little children can never tumble about in wild freedom on the cool grass in India, as they love so well to do at home. The deadly cobra di capello may be lurking there, and its bite is certain death. We have often felt sure that a very special providence alone preserved us from the many dangers by which we were surrounded. The snake being regarded by the Hindus as a god, no caste man will, on any account, kill even the most dangerous of them. But as our servants were generally *pariahs*, they would destroy them if a small reward were offered for every one they brought to us. One day, they called us out to see a long, green snake in the hedge, with a large bird in its mouth. It had first fascinated its poor victim, and was then greedily sucking its blood. The snake paid no attention to us, till some one threw a stone, when it glided swiftly down and concealed itself among the long, rank grass; but this species is not considered dangerous. We once saw an immense whip snake caught by a serpent charmer in our compound; but by far the most numerous there, were the deadly cobras. Several of these, when killed, measured five feet or more.

One morning we witnessed the critical and interesting operation of extracting the fangs of a large snake. It had been seen for several days about our kitchen garden, and a charmer was called to capture it, for our people could not. He soon succeeded in luring it out from among the large stones of the deep draw well. By producing a monotonous kind of music, not unlike the sound of the bagpipe, by blowing through a rude native instrument, he gradually drew it up to the outside of the verandah, where we stood. By a dexterous and sudden movement, the man passed his stick over it, and held its head tightly down to the ground, causing the cobra to open its venemous jaws. He then extracted with a pair of pincers the two teeth or fangs, which are in fact hollow tubes, communicating with the poison gland. Having pulled these out in our presence, the snake charmer next pressed the jaws of the serpent forcibly together, compelling it to eject the poison. He then presented a rag, at which the reptile snapped, and held fast. By this means the remains of the poison were wiped away, and the snake was rendered harmless. It was a very large and powerful cobra, yet the charmer seemed to have it under perfect control, and caused it to go through many singular movements, which it did, all the while distending its well marked hood.

One evening, my husband with his colleague were

seated together in the study, when something fell from the roof upon the head of the latter. Putting up his hand to ascertain what it was, he was severely stung by a scorpion. Not having the necessary remedy, they ran across the compound to the nearest house, to get the wound dressed. This done, they were about to return, when their friend kindly asked them to take a lantern. As it was but a few yards to their bungalow they thought it unnecessary, but on being pressed to do so, they accepted of it. And what was the gratitude of the two Missionaries when, on reaching the house, the light they carried fell upon a large snake stretched across the step of the verandah, upon which, in all probability, they must have trodden but for the kindly ray! Laying down the lantern, around which the serpent coiled itself, they procured sticks, and speedily despatched the dangerous visitor. A cobra once entered the native chapel at Mysore during the service, causing no small confusion and alarm. But a gracious Providence kept it from inflicting injury on any one.

Another adventure I can never forget. While sauntering along a little grassy walk behind the garden, a snake suddenly glided almost from under my feet. In my alarm, I sprang backwards, and the snake leaping in the same direction, it was close upon me again. Indeed, for a moment, I knew not which way to turn, and in my fright I could scarcely believe that I had not been bitten. Sometimes they would coil round the large flower pots along the edge of the outer verandah, and occasionally a cobra would enter a bath-room; but they rarely were found inside the house. The snake has, however, itself a mortal enemy in the long, lithe *mongoose*, another tenant of the Mission compound.

This little animal will fearlessly attack the deadly cobra, and it generally conquers in the fight. It was very interesting to watch the apparently unequal conflict, yet ending so satisfactorily.

Though not among the tenants of the compound, I must not leave out our first acquaintances, the Bangalore monkeys, already named in the first chapter. Round the native town, there was a thick *tope*, or grove, with an outer and inner mud wall around it; and here the monkeys reigned in undisturbed possession. Their courage and sagacity amused me not a little the first time I passed that way. They were there in hundreds, chasing, leaping, quarrelling, and swinging from tree to tree. Presently a dog that had followed us sprang forward, barking at them, and in an instant their fun was at an end, and they quickly formed into a fierce and warlike army. They hastily pushed all the mothers with their little ones down behind the inner wall; then mounting guard, they stood in a close line, quite ready for the fray. They gestured, showed their teeth, and uttered shrill, angry sounds, which I suppose were meant for shouts of defiance; but the enemy offered no further attack.

The old *munshi* used to tell us many stories about one cunning rogue, which had forced himself upon their charity as a daily pensioner. If they forgot to leave out his portion, the monkey would seize the first opportunity to dash into the house, and lay hold of the nearest article it could pounce upon. It then regularly seated itself on the house-top, holding the stolen property just in sight, till the owner, remembering his omission, hastily ran for its accustomed meal. One day, the *munshi* missed his treasured spectacles, and looking up, to his dismay saw the monkey flourishing them about in great triumph. Procuring a very tempting morsel, they laid it in the yard, calling, '*Timma, Timma,*' a name to which the monkey always answered, when it threw down the spectacles, and descending, helped itself to the feast with great relish.

But the best of all was the trick they played on the Commissioner himself. That gentleman, among other improvements in the *pettah,* wished to light up the main street, so he ordered a supply of tall lamps from England, in which cocoa-nut oil could be burned. In due time these arrived, and were set up, to the admiration of all. But the monkeys regarded them at first with grave suspicion. They carefully scanned them up and down from a distance; then venturing nearer by degrees, they at length mounted to the top, to see what was there. Sniffing the fragrant cocoa-nut oil inside, they watched their opportunity, and making a dash at the glass, they smashed several of the shades in endeavouring to feast upon the oil. The Commissioner was justly incensed, and ordered these daring thieves to be shot. The natives were horror-struck. What, shoot their gods! No, indeed; not for all the lamps in India. But at length an old Mussulman agreed to kill the monkeys for so much a head. Two fell, when immediately the whole tribe migrated to a wood several miles distant. Not one was left behind. The Hindus were filled with admiration, and chuckled with delight as they asked, 'Do you doubt any longer that they are gods, when they display such unheard of wisdom?' After the alarm had somewhat subsided, a few spies returned at short intervals to survey the land. Then small groups began to peer about their old haunts; and no molestation being offered, the entire community returned, and might be seen on every house-top, grinning and hungry as before. Finding that he could not destroy these mischievous animals without creating quite a disturbance among the natives, the Commissioner caused the monkeys to be captured and conveyed away in closely covered *bandies* or carts to a distant jungle, where they could indulge in their pranks without molesting any one.

I have by no means named all our welcome or unwelcome little neighbours, but these may suffice as giving a further glimpse of some of our common and very varied Indian experiences.

CHAPTER VIII.

DARK DAYS IN MISSION LIFE.

A HOT and oppressive March day is drawing to a close. The fiery sun has just gathered his beams around him, and has disappeared behind the horizon, when crowds of natives are seen hurrying from all sides to a wide, open space just outside the *pettah,* and in front of the Mysore Mission house. It is the night of the great *Sidhi habba,* or swinging feast, held every year in honour of Mari Amma. This cruel goddess is supposed to hold in her hand diseases of every kind. When she is offended, cholera or some other dreadful epidemic is let loose among the people. They at once seek to propitiate her by costly and bloody sacrifices almost without number. But in order to prevent the displeasure of this dreaded deity, three or four human victims offer themselves every year to undergo the tortures of the swinging feast, thus purchasing unbounded merit for themselves and the favour of the goddess for the thousands of their countrymen in Mysore.

For fifteen days before the festival begins, it is proclaimed through the town with beating of *tom-toms.* During this time, many processions of women and children may be seen going to lay their votive offerings upon Mari's shrine. These consist of fruit, flowers, cakes made of rice, sugar, and ghee, and also libations of oil. These things the offerers arrange neatly in small brass trays, and they place in the centre a burning lamp. They are then carried on the heads of the women, most of them having vowed to do so during times of sickness, and they are laid at the feet of the idol.

There are two temples in Mysore dedicated to this goddess of disease, and each of them had to be represented by a human victim at the annual swinging feast. Now the crowd becomes denser as the shadows deepen, while scores of blazing torches throw a restless lurid glare over all. Two cars containing the swinging machines, presently arrive on the spot we have named, just outside our gate. One, the male *sidhi*, is adorned with a tuft of peacock's feathers; and the other, the female *sidhi*, with flowers and branches. A tall, upright pole is securely fastened in the centre of the cars, and to each a cross-bar is attached. From these strong hooks are suspended, two to each bar.

The excitement now becomes intense. Devotees strike their gongs and bells, shouting aloud the names of their favourite gods; lights multiply, and the crowd sways backward and forward in breathless expectation. A fine young buffalo is then brought through the throng, and its head is struck off at a blow. Men, women, and children rush up with disgusting eagerness to catch the warm blood as it runs down from the headless trunk. Mothers rub it freely on their own foreheads, and besmear their infants with it, and fathers do the same. The two unhappy men who are to be the chief actors in this cruel drama, are now led up to the machines. Their naked backs have already been cut in two long gashes, one on each side of the backbone. This is done after the skin and muscles have been relaxed and prepared by rubbing with oil and frequent pulling. The hooks are then inserted, two in each victim, and the cross-bar is raised to the height of some forty feet. They are next swung round and round in the air, amid the plaudits of the excited multitude below. Three times the poor wretches meet in mid-air, when they make a feeble attempt at fencing with short wooden swords, which they hold in their hands.

Sick at heart, I hid myself in the innermost room of the Mission house; but escape I found none, for the shouts and cheers of the infatuated throng pursued me there. They fell like lead upon our spirits, and faith's wing seemed quite crippled, as we strove to lay their case before the Lord of the whole earth. The men were now taken down from their painful and perilous position. One groaned as if in great suffering, and the blood trickled from his gaping wounds. They were next conveyed to the fort, where the Rajah presented them with Cashmere shawls and jewels, while they were honoured and almost worshipped by the people. These men, it must be remembered, were willing and self-devoted victims. In times of distress, certain persons vow, that if they recover they will undergo this torture as a propitiatory offering to Mari, and every year, till this shameful exhibition of fanaticism was suppressed, there were several candidates ready to present themselves.

But now let us turn to another scene, in the freshness of early morning. A broad sheet of water forms a pleasing addition to the features of any landscape, but especially does it delight the eye in a hot and thirsty land like India. The great tank or lake at

Mysore soon after sunrise presented a pretty and ever varying picture of Eastern life, and all its surroundings were thoroughly oriental. Standing on the principal *bund,* or margin, we had on our left the fort and *pettah,* the palace being the central object on that side. Away on our extreme left towered sacred Çhamundi, covered with the aloe and cactus instead of the blooming heather that purpled the hills of old Scotland. Native gardens full of cocoa-nuts, areca palms, oranges, citrons, limes, and mango trees, with many others, completed the general surroundings of the principal tank. A wide flight of stone steps descended to the water's edge. Here a busy crowd were ever engaged, some bathing, some washing their long, flowing cloths by beating them on large stones, and others performing the various ceremonies connected with their morning devotions.

At a respectful distance from the comely and well-dressed Brahmans, you see a poor widow washing her only garment. One end of this she winds round her slight figure while she cleanses the other. Then fastening it to the branch of a tree or to a stone, she exposes it to the brilliant rays of the sun till it is dry, when she arranges it about her and walks away. Yonder, a great flock of buffaloes are revelling in the cool, refreshing water, the only parts visible being the very tops of their sleepy faces and the tips of their noses. Now a number of elephants, big and little, descend the green, sloping bank on our right, and with measured steps enter the tank to drink and to wash their dusty feet.

But turn again to the left, and look at the fine row of stately trees so thick and shady, encircled by small platforms of *chunam*. These have been planted as a work of merit by holy hands, to afford shade and rest for pilgrims. As we approach them, and at the same time cast a glance up to the proud pagoda that crowns the high hill Chamundi, we are strikingly reminded of that text, 'And they set them up images and groves in every high hill, and under every green tree' (2 Kings xvii. 10); for under each leafy bough are reared many idols, conspicuous among them being stone representations of the serpent god. Here worshippers, male and female, are performing their devotions. One desires the blessing of health, another gold, and a third asks for a son to perpetuate the family name and maintain its honour. Round and round they walk with folded hands, laying at each turn a flower, a lime, or a mango before the idol.

In southern India there are two monsoons,—the early rains, setting in in June, and the latter, in October. The health and prosperity of the people greatly depend on the regularity of these, for with the exception of the mango showers in April, little, if any, rain falls during the rest of the year. The monsoons of 1863 had partially failed. Month after month of 1864 also passed without a drop of rain to water the thirsty earth. The fierce rays of a scorching sun streamed down from a cloudless sky, till the ground was parched and rent as we had never seen it before. Victims had suffered all the tortures of the swinging feast I have described to bring down a blessing on the people, but it was very evident to us that a cloud of Divine wrath was gathering over the city instead.

The great tank was no longer the morning resort of cheerful and busy crowds. It had become so shallow and stagnant as to be quite unfit for all ordinary purposes. Worse still, the wells in the *pettah* were now dry, and the Corinzie Tank, so much smaller and more distant than the other, contained the only scanty supply of drinkable water in or near Mysore. One of the first duties of a Hindu wife is to fetch water for the day's use from the well near her house. With their brightly polished *jumboos*, or vessels, on their heads or under their arms, the women often assemble in cheerful groups, and display more activity in getting their supply drawn up than they usually do. But at the time I am now describing it was sad indeed to watch the long line of men, women, and children toiling twice a day along that hot and dusty road with their heavy burdens. Bullocks, too, with leathern bottles filled with the precious fluid slung across their backs like panniers, mingled with the throng, and moved slowly along towards the fort and *pettah*. But so alarmingly low and muddy had even the Corinzie become from the incessant demand upon it, that the people had to strain the water through cloths before they could pour it into their vessels.

Few, we think, who have lived amid times of drought and famine in an Eastern land, and have witnessed the distress caused by lack of water, will ever be able to waste it again with a quiet conscience. Trees that had borne the sun's directer ray during many a year stood black and bare, seemingly burnt up for want of moisture. We saw many noble specimens in this state in the Rajah's orchard. Cholera had already broken out in several parts of the city, and the people in terror daily besought the Rajah to bring rain. The poor old King had been using every means but the right one to do so, and had given large sums of money to the Brahmans to pray constantly to their gods for the much-needed monsoon.

Just at this juncture there came a holy sage one day to the court. Obtaining an early interview with the Rajah, the stranger agreed to bring rain within three weeks, provided he should receive one thousand five hundred rupees, or £150, as his reward. If he failed to perform his promise, he vowed that at the end of the stipulated time he should break off his sacred thread,—the peculiar badge of all Brahmans,—and become an outcast. The Rajah agreed to his conditions, so the wonder-worker at once betook himself to his task. Day after day, however, passed without result. The heavens were still as brass. As the three weeks wore away, the rainmaker became more frantic in his efforts to draw down the desired boon on the parched land. Daily he ascended to the top of the great pagoda, that he might watch and direct the clouds; and he vowed that if rain did not fall soon he would commit suicide. About the end of the stipulated three weeks, the descent of a refreshing shower raised his spirits and those of the expectant and eager throngs who watched the holy man. But as the monsoon did not set in then, the Rajah dismissed the sage, with handsome presents of cloths, jewels, and other things to the value of five hundred rupees.

The crops of that year failing, signs of scarcity and even of famine soon followed. The prices of provisions rose so rapidly that the poor began to suffer very severely. The lower classes in southern India depend for the most part on the supply of a coarse, black grain called *ragi* for their daily food. It is much cheaper than rice, and a meal of this, pounded and made into a kind of thick pudding will, they say, stand by them all day long, while a meal of rice is gone directly. As money grew scarcer, *ragi* was more than ever sought after, but at length the supply altogether failed. A report became current that a number of wealthy grain merchants, anticipating the approach of famine, had concealed large stores under their shops. The excitement of the people was intense; and one Sabbath a distant and confused murmur, as of a vast multitude or the far off roar of the ocean, reached the Mission house. The Rajah's sepoys and a crowd of eager followers had conspired to burst open the shops of the merchants, and were then busily engaged in looting the bazaar.

My husband was quite distressed by the prayers, importunities, and even tears of the people every time he went into the *pettah*. He was so well known there, that many flocked to him for help in their trouble as to a tried friend. He often failed to recognise in the emaciated creatures who were most clamorous for assistance the faces of some with whom he was perfectly familiar but a short time before.

One morning the tidings that a large number of carts filled with *ragi* had just come to town caused al faces to brighten. Among others, most of our native Christians, who were suffering much from the want of their accustomed food, flocked to the spot. All the day long they stood patiently in the midst of the hungry multitude, holding their bags in one hand, and their money in the other, anxiously awaiting their turn to come; but they waited in vain. The clamorous crowd nearest to the temporary barrier that had been put up to keep them off could bridle their impatience no longer; they burst through, and helped themselves freely to all the grain that remained.

It was a bitter disappointment to our poor people. They came to us with sad faces and tearful eyes, holding out their empty bags, and asked pitifully, '*Ayàh*, how can we go home without food to our poor wives and hungry little children?' We could not bear to see this state of things any longer; so selecting a few able-bodied Christian men, we sent them away to the *ragi* district, many miles distant, ordering them to bring us a *bandy* load at any price. Earnestly praying for the success of their expedition, we saw them go forth. God prospered them on their somewhat hazardous journey, and they returned with radiant faces and a full cart. Our storeroom was immediately turned into a granary, and the pure delight we experienced in measuring out the grain to our suffering people I cannot express.

Among those who came for a supply, was a bigoted old heathen man, the father of one of our young Christians. He had sternly opposed his son, and in every way sought to prevent him from taking the decisive step. But finding his authority insufficient to keep his son from publicly confessing Christ, the mortified father had bitterly accused my husband of being their enemy. As he now handed the old idolater a full basket, he smilingly asked, 'Do you think I hate you now?' It was too much for the now humbled man. His face quivered with emotion as he said, '*Ayàh*, that word has pierced my heart.'

The Rajah was much distressed by the troubles of his subjects, and did all he could to lessen them. He caused a large booth to be erected in an open space by the Market Street, and there hundreds received one meal of rice daily in charity. Passing this place one morning, on my way to the *pettah* school, I saw an object I can never forget. Within a few yards of the school door lay the fearfully emaciated form of a man in the last stage of starvation. Hearing that food could be obtained in Mysore, the poor fellow had crawled with extreme difficulty to this place; but nature was utterly exhausted, and, in sight of the booth, he had laid himself down to die. The condition of that wasted frame was indescribably sad to witness. The man was literally a breathing skeleton. Sick at heart, I ran forward to our small book depository, and hastily sent our *colporteur*, Daniel, to help him and try to feed him. But, alas! help had come too late. The weary wheels of life were just standing still, and in a faint whisper the poor sufferer could only entreat Daniel to leave him alone to die.

Oh how we watched and prayed for rain! Every day for weeks the clouds gathered, but at noon a high wind always rose and scattered them. The seed time was rapidly wearing past, and the people said if the rain did not set in very soon, nothing but death was before them. It is one thing to read or hear of famine at a distance, but quite another to be in the midst of it. Though the Missionaries had all their wants supplied, and never endured the pangs of hunger themselves, yet we suffered intensely in witnessing so much distress that we were powerless to alleviate. As is so often the case pestilence too, the grim sister of famine, was now abroad in the city; and many fell smitten on every side, as by the touch of the destroying angel. It was a season of dread and dismay to such as had no hiding place for a time of trouble, and no certain hope beyond the reach of the spoiler.

Processions of every kind were formed, and passed along the streets daily. The Roman Catholics, with crucifix and banners; the Mohamedans, with their sacred koran covered with lace, and borne high on the back of a camel, promenaded the city, with music, chanting, and burning of sweet incense. Chamundeshwari, the patron goddess of the palace, was brought down from her mountain temple, and amid the booming of cannon—a royal salute being fired in honour of her descent—was carried in a silver palanquin through the fort and *pettah* with unwonted pomp. Many bloody sacrifices were offered. Balls of rice, mingled with the blood, were thrown in the air, with cries to the offended deity; but that mysterious disease, which so truly 'walketh in darkness,' still continued to rage. Close to the end wall of our compound there was a small devil temple. Round this place the people used to assemble towards midnight, and with clanging of bells, striking of gongs, and the most unearthly yells, they strove to affright the evil spirits. It was unspeakably awful in a time of pestilence to be roused from one's slumbers at dead of night by such horrid sounds as almost chilled our blood. It seemed to us as if the madness of those wretched idolaters must continue to draw down upon them the signal vengeance of high Heaven.

Yet strange to say, amid all these scenes of fanaticism and terror, the people turned to the Missionary as to a true friend. At his hand very many thankfully received the medicine, which no persuasion would induce them to take from the kind English doctor of the station. Too often, a native finding himself attacked by cholera, at once lies down to die. Fate, as written in his forehead, has ordained it so, he believes; and so, without a rational effort to arrest the progress of this dire disease, he soon sinks under it. But many friends of the sufferers hastened to the Mission house in their trouble, and not a few, by God's blessing on the use of the remedies we employed, recovered.

For a time the members of our little Church escaped; but at length a fine young man, an aged widow's only son, sickened and died. The funeral was to take place the next afternoon, and arrangements were made accordingly. On reaching the house of mourning, however, my husband found the bereaved mother in the greatest distress and consternation. Owing to the intense heat of that oppressive and trying season, decomposition had already commenced; and the *coolies*, or bearers, who had been hired to carry the bier had all fled in alarm. No one could be prevailed upon for money to expose themselves to so great danger of infection. The Missionary comprehended the state of things at a glance. There was not a moment to be lost; so remounting his horse, he hastened home at full speed. Calling all our servants—of whom we are compelled to keep several in India, as caste forbids a man to do more than one department of work—he asked them, as a personal favour, to go along with him and stand by him in this painful emergency. To their honour, be it said, not one of them refused. Animated by the example of their master, and encouraged by his cheering words, the men took up the bier, and speedily conveyed it to the place of sepulture. On reaching the graveyard, however, great was their consternation to find that the grave was only partially dug. Owing to the delay that had already occurred, the sun was now near his setting, and the state of the corpse rendered further exposure most dangerous; so throwing off his coat, my dear husband jumped into the grave, and soon completed the sad and unusual work.

Mission life is invested with little romance in such hours as these. As all the servants had gone with their master, I was left quite alone as the shadows deepened. It was only by nestling closely under the covert of the Almighty wing that one could feel calm and secure under these circumstances, or rise above such painful scenes and surroundings. Some of our servants were still heathen, so I met them with a warm welcome on their return, assuring them that the Christian's God could preserve them from harm, as easily in the midst of extreme danger as in times of happiness and safety. God did graciously shield both us and them, for the plague was not permitted to come nigh our dwelling.

One day as we sat at dinner we suddenly heard the quick, heavy patter of large raindrops. The table was deserted in an instant, and, will my young reader smile when I own, that in our ecstasy, we ran out in the midst of it, just like children, actually to *feel* it? Yes; in the midst of much deserved wrath, our Father God had remembered mercy. The monsoon had burst upon us at last. Soon the lurid lightnings and the terrific thunderclaps relieved the stagnant atmosphere and unsealed the clouds, causing them to drop fatness on the hard and barren earth once more. Sickness soon abated, and ere long health and a measure of prosperity began to return to the city.

THE RAJAH OF MYSORE.

CHAPTER IX.

THE NATIVE COURT OF MYSORE.

AN Eastern court is always surrounded by much external pomp, glitter, and gaudy show. Most native princes strive to increase their dignity and renown by gathering around them a host of learned pundits, holy sages, sycophants, and idle retainers. Not a few can boast of a magnificent *zenana*, or *harem*, also, where many a dark-eyed beauty languishes in weary luxurious ease and captivity. These are waited upon by a crowd of handmaidens and eunuchs, and on them the vulgar gaze of the outside world may never fall.

We were not likely to forget that Mysore was a royal city, for it could boast of not fewer than four palaces. The oldest and most important of these was situated within the fort, and here the Rajah himself resided. The next, but really the handsomer and more substantial of the two, was built not many years ago, chiefly for the purpose of entertaining European visitors, when the Rajah should receive back his kingdom. It stood in a prominent position in the *pettah*, and was sumptuously furnished in English style, with a dash of gay Eastern decoration blending through all. The walls of the dining and reception halls were adorned with large paintings of the Rajah's sacred and favourite cows, with their calves. The third was the pleasure palace. Its gateway was very handsome and imposing, and the grounds and garden were prettily laid out.

They contaiued a good labyrinth built of *chunam*, with a small tower in the centre. In this palace was kept an amusing variety of movable pictures, mechanical curiosities, and ornaments of all kinds, for which a fabulous price had been paid, as the Rajah was known to be very fond of collecting such things. The fourth palace was erected about the time of our arrival in Mysore, on the high ground outside the town, at the request, it was said, of a favourite concubine.

On the defeat and death of the cruel and vindictive Tippoo, and the overthrow of his dynasty, in 1799, the representative of the ancient family of the Rajahs of Mysore was sought out by the British government. Krishna Rajah Wudier Bohadoor was then a child, according to some writers of three, and others, five years of age. As his mother died soon after his birth, he was then living with his grandparents and aunt, in deep poverty and obscurity. Mysore, the former capital, was selected as his place of residence; and the little Rajah was placed upon the throne, in the presence of a vast throng of Hindus, amid deafening plaudits and great rejoicings. The young sovereign was, in many respects, a most amiable prince, and under judicious training he might have become a wise and good ruler. But cradled and brought up as he was, in the midst of ignorance, superstition, and servile flattery, one can scarcely wonder that he soon became the dupe of unprincipled and designing men. This eventually led to his being deprived of all political power, though he still retained his title.

We shall now return to the first palace, within the fort. It was a large, very oriental-looking building, forming three sides of a square. Balconies, gaily painted and gilded, supported by many carved pillars, adorned the lofty front. Underneath these was the great arched gateway leading into the inner courtyard. Visitors always dismounted outside this, where they were received by the prime minister. Soon after our arrival in Mysore we paid our first visit to the Rajah, who was then an old man. Mr. Hodson accompanied us, and two carriages with outriders and runners were sent to convey us to the palace. We arrived, by appointment, a little before sunset. Passing through the grand ontrance, we were conducted along many narrow lobbies and staircases, which were by no means elegant or remarkably clean. In crossing one of these, we had a sight of the Rajah's sacred horse. It was kept as an object of worship, and it had the honour to occupy a room at one end of the lower hall. It was a gentle and beautiful creature, of the very highest breed, and its eyes were the finest I ever saw an animal possessed of. I saw it once during the *Dasuri* feast, standing under a booth erected on the *bund* of the great tank, guarded by a company of soldiers, and surrounded by a large crowd of worshippers. It was magnificently jewelled and caparisoned; and so was the sacred elephant, which occupied another booth behind. Every morning and evening while that feast lasted they were brought out to receive the adoration of the people. The horse seemed as if he realised his exalted position, for he arched his proud neck and bowed his noble head to the admiring throng, now advancing, now retreating, to the evolutions of the dancing girls. The Rajah's sacred cows also occupied apartments in the palace. One of these, we were gravely informed, was led into the state bedroom early every morning, that the Rajah's eyes might first rest upon it on his awaking, as this insured an auspicious day.

We were received by His Highness on the house-top, which was carpeted, and round the sides couches and chairs were nicely arranged. He had come up to enjoy the evening breeze, and courteously advanced to meet us, handing me to a chair. While conversing with the Missionaries, he said thoughtfully, 'Yes; Jesus Christ must have been more than man, else He never could have established such a religion.' Yet the aged Rajah was a confirmed idolater. Being a great patron of native learning, his court was always thronged by a crowd of the most arrogant Brahmans. They had secured a complete ascendency over him, and this they were very jealous to maintain, as it paid them well. He spent in gifts to these, immense sums of money, as well as in securing further merit by building temples. He was an implicit believer in astrology, and spent much time in its study. Without consulting the stars, he would commence no undertaking, nor make any engagement, however trifling.

As they sat talking on various subjects, I had leisure to look round at the beautiful fancy pigeons in their cribs beside us. In doing so, my eye fell on that wing of the palace beneath us on the left, which I knew at a glance must be the *zenana*. Many dark eyes from its high windows were peering curiously at us, and many jewelled hands began eagerly to beckon for me to go to them. How I longed to do so! but of course I could not without the invitation of their lord. Some years later the much desired request came. I was to visit the royal ladies along with Mrs. Elliot, the excellent wife of the Resident at Mysore. An early day was named, but, alas! the stars fought against us. An astrologer made the important discovery that just then an unlucky planet would be in the ascendant, and our visit was postponed. Before the favourable day came, we had started on a journey which could not be delayed.

Poor prisoners! I pitied them most sincerely. Without the power to beguile the weary hours by reading or needlework, and with none of the light domestic duties of most *zenana* occupants, no wonder if jealousy and quarrels were sadly common. They rarely went abroad, and then they were carried in closely-curtained palanquins, in which holes just large enough for the eye were embroidered. Occasionally we met the procession, as they were slowly borne along up the thousand stone steps cut out of the solid granite rock of the hill Chamundi. Here they went at intervals to worship Chamundéshwari, the patron goddess of the palace, in her handsome and much frequented temple at the top. They generally returned after sunset by torch light. On state occasions, these 'guarded treasures' were permitted to stand in a gallery, closely concealed by curtains perforated with small embroidered holes, as in their palanquins. Through these they peeped at all that went on, taking notice of everything and every person. These were red letter days to the inmates of the *zenana*, for they could never leave it but by special permission. Indeed, report said that this suite of apartments was closed in by a massive door with silver padlock, of which only the Rajah kept the key.

The old king thoroughly respected the position occupied by Missionaries among the other Europeans in India. While he invited us to his birthday *durbars* and to similar select festivals, yet he never on any occasion asked us to attend an entertainment connected with races or with idolatry. Now, would our young friends like to have a glimpse of an Eastern *durbar?* We shall first select as a fair specimen that held on the occasion of the Rajah completing his seventieth year. He was the oldest prince in India.

At a quarter past seven p.m. we drove up to the appointed place of meeting, where we were joined by a long procession of torch-bearers, spearmen, and horsemen. Headed by the carriage of the Commissioner, we formed into line and entered the fort, where we were welcomed by a thundering salute from the guns on the ramparts. The streets along which we passed were railed in by bamboos decked with flowers, and on them were placed rows of small lamps the whole way. As we drove up to the palace, the band struck up the national anthem, and dismounting we were received by the prime minister just outside the grand entrance. Coloured lamps gleamed from every niche, balcony, and pillar. Elephants with silver *houdahs*, and companies of the Sillidar horse, with finely equipped riders, were drawn up on either side; while in front a large triumphal arch had been erected in honour of the occasion. We were led up flights of stairs and along narrow passages crowded with officials, to the great *durbar* or reception hall.

Here a dazzling and truly oriental scene burst upon us. It reminded me rather of a picture from the *Arabian Nights' Entertainments* than a reality. The room, with its vaulted roof all carved and gilded, was a perfect blaze of light. Handsome prism-hung chandeliers were suspended in every direction. Galleries supported by richly decorated pillars and arches ran all round the place. These were profusely adorned with mirrors, coloured lamps, and lustres. In the middle of the hall, as its central ornament, an octagonal frame was arranged. Inside and outside of this small, brilliant lamps were placed in the form of a star, and in the midst rose a pale blue glass pedestal, on which stood a large silver ball. Here the fairy-like scene was mirrored, the bright uniforms of the English officers adding to the effect of the whole.

On a handsome chair at the farther end of the room sat the Rajah. At an earlier *durbar* we had seen him seated on a magnificent silver throne, with canopy and fringe of silver. This stood on a carpet of cloth of gold. He wore a turban of pale blue and silver, richly jewelled, as were his cuffs, wrists, fingers, and slippers. Around him clustered a crowd of attendants. Some of those approached from time to time to receive his commands, with hands clasped and raised as to a divinity; and others bowed to the ground before their King. One gently fanned his sacred person with a large gilded fan, while two more waved crimson feathery fly brushes to ward off unwary mosquitoes, and a fourth held the indispensable casket of *betel* leaf, which all the natives of India incessantly chew. Heralds at intervals loudly proclaimed the titles and glories of their sovereign; and at the other end of the hall, dancing girls, magnificently attired and almost covered with gold and gems, performed a succession of not ungraceful movements with hands and feet. On entering we all passed before the Rajah, and shook hands as the Resident introduced each by name. When all were seated, a pretty little boy, the adopted son and future heir to the throne of Mysore, was brought in, and presented to us in the arms of an attendant. He was dressed in military costume, with turban and tiny sword. But the sight of so many white faces and glittering uniforms was too much for the little three years' old hero. He had to be hastily taken away to more congenial society, though a few years later this prince behaved among strangers with all the dignity of a king.

After taking leave of the Rajah, the Commissioner led the way to the spacious dining-hall. Here a sumptuous dinner, consisting of almost every variety of fish, flesh, and fowl that can be procured in southern India, was served up, with curries and sweets in great profusion. The number of cooks employed and sums expended on these occasions were extraordinary. The guests numbered more than eighty, and we were waited on by a host of attendants so numerous that they jostled against each other, and crowded most inconveniently around. The inexorable laws of caste forbade the Rajah being present during dinner; but on dessert being placed on the table, he was brought in by the Commissioner and Resident, when the health of the Queen and then that of our host was proposed. He now rose and escorted us to a balcony overlooking the courtyard, where a display of fireworks was going on. A tame horse and elephant performed several feats, while green, red, and white lights were thrown up with singular effect. The Rajah then conducted his guests to another open hall, where further entertainments were provided. At a given time, the prime minister and attendants approached with garlands, bouquets, and a golden flask containing otto of roses.

The Commissioner placed a wreath round the neck of the Rajah, after which each of the company was similarly adorned, and presented with a bouquet and a shower of perfume. We then took leave of our hospitable entertainer, returning home about eleven p.m.

Such occasions were not the most congenial to us as Missionaries; but as the old King so considerately invited us only to his most select and unobjectionable gatherings, we could not refuse to pay our respects to him. We were old residents at Mysore, and our absence would have been regarded as a personal slight.

We once had the honour of being present at the palace on an occasion of special interest. This was the formal presentation of a number of beautiful gifts from Her Majesty Queen Victoria to the Rajah. Carriages were in waiting at noon to convey us to the residency, where we first assembled. The road from this to the palace in the fort was lined by Sillidar horse, their riders wearing bright new uniforms; that of the officers was heavy with gold embroidery. A company of these formed the vanguard of the procession, which now formed, and another brought up the rear. Several immense elephants, bearing massive silver *houdahs*, went first. Their huge limbs, trunks, and tusks were gaily painted with such wonderful flowers as never grew even in that land of gaudy blossoms. Handsome coverings of cloth of gold were thrown over them, reaching almost to the ground; while jewels, tassels, and floral wreaths were suspended from their necks. The Commissioner and Resident mounted the *houdah* of the great elephant, when the procession moved off. Two baby elephants, followed by a number of camels, came next; then about thirty carriages with outriders.

These were surrounded and followed by standard and insignia bearers, with spearmen and horsemen, including the Rajah's own bodyguard. Of course, *tom-toms* and music were there in abundance, without which no Eastern procession would be complete.

We proceeded to the palace by a circuitous route through vast crowds, who thronged both streets and house-tops. The Rajah received us in the lower *durbar* hall standing, a very unusual honour, and shook hands with all. He was handsomely dressed in full uniform, blue and scarlet, richly embroidered with gold. A costly necklace of emeralds, with large clusters of pearls, adorned his neck; and at his side hung a valuable sword in scabbard of crimson velvet, studded with gold and emeralds. This was a gift on a former occasion from our Queen. The Rajah seated himself by the side of an elaborately-carved silver throne, while we sat wondering why it was left unoccupied. Presently a large royal carriage drove into the court-yard, and drew up in front of the open hall, where we sat waiting. This contained the presents, which were all unfolded that we might see them. The Commissioner and every one now rose, and remained standing while he, in a graceful address, presented the gifts to His Highness in the name of the Queen. He then handed to the Rajah a casket of solid silver, which contained beautiful miniatures of the Prince and Princess of Wales. This was placed with great ceremony on the vacant throne, as representing her majesty, the old King making at the same time a profound *salaam*.

A salver containing rose leaves mixed with fragments of gold leaf was then handed to him, and these he sprinkled over all the presents, which were now piled round the throne. He next took two salvers filled with rupees—two shilling pieces—and after waving them over his gifts, the Rajah handed them to the Commissioner and Resident to scatter among the soldiers and others, who thronged every nook and corner of the courtyard. As the silver shower descended over the heads of the people, the most frantic efforts were made by a forest of outstretched hands to catch it. Again and again the salvers were replenished, till one thousand five hundred rupees were scattered among them, the excitement meanwhile becoming almost alarming. At length a fine English officer with stentorian lungs succeeded in creating a sudden lull in the tempest. In a moment the soldiers formed into columns, and fired a ringing volley of three times three. The usual concluding ceremony of receiving garlands, betel leaf, bouquets, and perfume having been performed, we took leave of the Rajah, and returned home as we came in grand procession.

My young readers may be curious to know of what the gifts consisted. There were several elegant velvet table-covers, richly inwrought with gold, some valuable curiosities, of which the Rajah was particularly fond, and the casket, besides some beautiful albums, silks, and moire-antiques for the ladies of the *zenana*.

Just before our return to England in 1867 we went to take leave of the old gentleman, who received us most kindly and without ceremony. From his increasing feebleness we feared that we might never on earth see him again, and so it proved. On our return to Mysore two years and a half later, the pretty young Rajah, Cham Rajendra Wudier, occupied his throne, and the aged king had gone—ah, whither? A short time after we left he became dangerously ill. His physicians were summoned, and gold was freely offered to purchase relief. One of them seemed to understand the nature of his malady, and prepared a cordial, which relieved the royal sufferer. Many valuable gifts of jewels, money, and other things were at once heaped upon the fortunate doctor. But the unfavourable symptoms soon returned, and it became evident to all that the dread conqueror, before whom prince and peasant alike must bow, had entered the palace. 'Is there no one among all the thousands of my dependants in this city who can help me now?' piteously exclaimed the dying Rajah. Again a cordial was administered which gave temporary relief, and for this five hundred rupees were paid. On recovering consciousness, he called for his adopted son, then a fine boy of about five years of age. The dying king affectionately kissed the young prince, and handed him his royal sword and rings, with his blessing. His wives were then permitted to say farewell. As they stood around his couch the sufferer spoke a few kind words to them, while they wept and lamented. They were then commanded immediately to return to the *zenana*.

In India, the luxury of a soft dying couch is denied to the fainting frame. Were the dying one to expire on a bed, or even on a mat, the spirit would, they believe, enter its new body carrying this encumbrance along with it. As death was now rapidly approaching, the poor old Rajah was carried down from his comfortable chamber, and laid upon a little straw on the ground-floor to die. The strange and revolting ceremonies by which a Hindu's soul and body are supposed to be cleansed from all defilement, were then strictly performed; nor were liberal presents to the Brahmans—an essential accompaniment of every rite—forgotten. From time to time they moistened his parched lips with the holy water of the Ganges. Twelve Brahmans stood around, calling upon the names of their favourite gods, 'Rama, Rama, Krishna, Shiva, Narahyana,' while the dying Rajah feebly uttered the name of his own deity, 'Hari, Hari,' as long as he had strength left to articulate. Thus, at a little before midnight, he passed into the darkness, with no light to chase the deepest gloom of the valley away, and no golden beams of a brighter dawn beyond breaking on the distant horizon.

The next morning, as the city awoke from its slumbers, the booming of seventy-four minute guns announced to the people that their king was dead, and not a few seemed really to mourn sincerely for him. A strange custom prevails in India in connection with the funeral ceremonies, which to European eyes is most repugnant. The corpse is dressed up in handsome clothing, and gaily adorned with jewels and garlands of flowers. It is then placed in a chair or palanquin in a sitting posture; and in this way it is carried to the grave or funeral pile, according to the caste of the departed. I shall not soon forget the shock I once had, on meeting a showy procession of this kind. I recognised at a glance that ghastly face, with its glazed eyes, as that of one of our best heathen teachers, who had died suddenly but a few hours before. It seemed such a solemn mockery of death.

The deceased Rajah was speedily arrayed in gorgeous apparel, and adorned with the most costly gems, such as rubies, diamonds, &c. He was then placed in a magnificent palanquin, which was also ornamented with jewels and gold. The widowed queens now took their last look of their husband, and the procession moved slowly on to the mausoleum in the royal gardens. The sacred horse, elephant, and cow, divested of all their gay trappings, were there as mourners, along with a vast crowd of many thousands. From time to time as they passed along a salute was fired by the sepoys, and handfuls of money were thrown among the people.

The procession now entered the garden, where a grand funeral pile, composed of the fragrant and valuable sandal-wood mingled with camphor, was in readiness. The royal corpse was gently laid upon it, and it was lighted up. The flames soon did their work, and a few charred bones were all that remained of the old Rajah. These were taken to the holy city Benares to be thrown into the sacred river Ganges, and the ashes were carefully collected and sent to Seringapatam, to mingle with the waters of the celebrated river Cavery.

THE NUNJINGODE TEMPLE.

CHAPTER X.

THE SACRED SHRINE.

INDIA literally teems with holy persons, places, and things. There are sacred trees, sacred shrubs, and sacred flowers. There are sacred mountains too, to gain whose summit and worship there is to gain a title to heaven. There are sacred rivers, in whose purifying waters the sin of the soul can be as easily washed away as the defilement of the body; and there are sacred animals, birds, and reptiles, which receive worship and homage without stint from the multitude. Nor are sacred shrines wanting in that land of 'gods many.' Some of these are small, and but little frequented, while others attract many thousands of pilgrims every year.

The most celebrated Shivite place of worship in the Mysore territory is Nunjingode. The name means, 'the house of the drinker of poison.' It is given to Shiva, because their *puràna*s tell that he drank the poison first produced by churning the milk sea, when the gods were in quest of ambrosia. Worshippers flock to this holy shrine from all quarters, and many come a distance of several hundred miles to pay their vows there, and to bathe in the sacred waters of the Capila. This they believe to be the surest and shortest way to obtain purity and heaven.

The sun had just risen on a bright October morning, when we started to visit this famous temple. The dewdrops yet sparkled on the leaves, and the soft breeze that just stirred them was cool and refreshing. Now we were passing a plantation of waving sugar cane, then a plantain or banana garden, next a field of the purple-stalked castor-oil plant, with its rough green berries, and again a clump of palm trees, with their yellow scaly trunks and feathery tops. To several of these small earthen vessels called *chatties* were attached, in order to catch the juice that oozes from them after they have been punctured. This is called *toddy*, which is frequently drunk by the natives of India after fermentation. It is then intoxicating. As we drew near to the town of Nunjingode we passed group after group of pilgrims, all bound for the same goal. Aged men and women were there, toiling along, weary and foot-sore, in hope of gaining merit enough to purchase happiness and heaven at the end of the day, which was already far spent with some of them. Fathers, with their children astride their shoulders, hastened onward too, the mothers with their babes on their side following at a respectful distance. Now we met a long line of more than a hundred native *bandies*, or carts, drawn by bullocks. These were bound for Mysore, to which they were conveying government money. At length, a turn of the road brought us full in sight of the Capila, whose bright waters wind about like links of molten silver in the dazzling sunlight. Nunjingode, with its far-famed temple, is built in one of the bends of the river. After crossing a bridge with an immense number of arches, we entered the little town, and at once proceeded to a grove of mango and other trees, leaving our horse and conveyance under the grateful shade. We then walked up towards the temple, whose two grand pagodas stood out in bold relief against the cloudless sky.

We had not gone far, when our attention was arrested by the movements and appearance of a native lady. She was a Brahmani, evidently belonging to a superior family—the female members of which are so seldom to be seen outside the walls of the *zenana.* She looked young, almost a girl, and she was very beautiful. Her slight, graceful form was becomingly draped in a flowing garment of rich silk. The only jewels she wore were a pair of elegant gold ear pendants, and one massive necklace of the same adorned her neck. At first, we had no idea what she was doing; but the wistful sadness of her lovely dark eyes and chiselled features made us stand to watch her. We soon saw that she was engaged in the performance of a vow. Beginning at the brink of the river, she turned round and prostrated herself at full length on the ground, at every step laying her head in the dust. A little boy, probably her son, though she looked too young to be his mother, carefully imitated her every movement. She had come, we were told, from Mysore, as a last hope, with her husband, who was sick, apparently unto death. He was then lying in the porch of the temple, while his beautiful young wife strove, by performing this wearisome and humiliating penance, to avert the fatal blow.

Sad indeed is such a bereavement in this land of Bibles, with all the balm for wounded hearts, and all the bright immortal hopes of our glorious Christianity. But to become a widow in India is to become a reproach and curse, an object of contempt and shame. Poor girl! well might she dread that crushing stroke!

No matter how faithfully she had striven to serve and please her husband, no matter at what cost she had sought to alleviate his sufferings and save his life, his death would be attributed by all to her sins in a former birth. The younger she is now, the greater a sinner she must have been before, to draw down this judgment so early upon her. Such is the only word of sympathy that will meet her ear. No friend will seek to soothe or share her sorrow, no finger will point her to the God in whose great heart of love the widow and the fatherless find a *peculiar* place. No; her long glossy tresses will be shaven off, the dim, scanty, cotton cloth—the widow's badge—will be put on, and a life of misery and insult will immediately begin. Oh! how I wanted to draw her to my side, and tell her of Him whose ear is ever open to the cry of the needy, and whose touch can bring healing to diseased souls, as well as to sick bodies! I approached her, but her eye never once glanced at me. It appeared riveted to that one sacred spot, in which her suffering husband and his god were placed so near to each other.

Leaving the beautiful girl to finish her self-imposed task, which we were powerless to prevent, we pressed forward, with saddened hearts, to the great frowning gateway of the temple. Surmounted by two elaborately sculptured pagodas, with richly gilded horns on the top, the temple itself is an immense square, with an open court in the centre. The four sides are filled with the shrines of innumerable deities. Outside these runs a wide verandah supported by many columns. Over this is a highly ornamental coping, and the spaces between the pillars contain sculptured niches filled with figures of every kind. To attempt to describe these is quite impossible. Some are curious, some meaningless, many are grotesque, while others are so *vile* that I dared not even glance at them. And yet this is one of India's most holy shrines! On these detestable objects, innocent little children, boys and girls, youths and maidens, gaze with eager eyes; as well as those with furrowed brows and hoary hairs. They listen to all the loose and profane remarks such carvings readily suggest, and they neither shudder nor blush. Do not their parents smile at such things, and are they not sanctioned by their gods? Oh, how differently would Christian men and women estimate the needs of poor India, could they watch the folly and fanaticism of these excited multitudes, and understand something of what is said and done at such places under the name of religion!

At each full moon the great god of this temple, Shiva, is brought out, mounted on a silver bull, and carried about in procession. But it is in the month of March that the greatest of all the festivals is celebrated at Nunjingode. The feast lasts for fifteen days, when it is estimated that not fewer than forty thousand persons assemble in the place. The great car, a huge and unwieldy structure many tiers high, and covered with carved figures similar to those on the temple, is brought out, and gaily decorated with banners and streamers. This belongs to the god Shiva and his wife. Two smaller ones, similarly decked up, are dedicated to their two sons. Servants, elephants, horses, and ornaments used to be supplied by the late Rajah of Mysore, who also built, at great cost, the chief *pagoda* of the temple. Many rich gifts were also sent by him every year. As soon as the large car was drawn along by dint of tremendous effort, tidings were instantly despatched to him in the city, when he caused a salute to be fired in honour of the auspicious event.

But it is time now to return to the great gateway of the temple, at which we took our stand. A busy scene was going on around us, though this was not a special occasion. In the courtyard many small vessels, containing incense, sent up tiny, snowy clouds of sweet perfume into the clear blue sky. Worshippers were continually entering with offerings of fruit and flowers, or oblations of honeyed water, milk, and *ghee*, with which to bathe the idol. A tame elephant walked about, picking up with its trunk the plantain and other leaves thrown down in the court by the offerers. Round the gate sat holy *sanyasies*, or devotees, their naked and emaciated bodies entirely covered with ashes. Religious mendicants, too, were there, big, sturdy fellows, with their fantastic turbans composed of stripes of all kinds of showy materials, and adorned by tufts of feathers. They looked as if they throve on their profession, and seemed to enjoy life. They held gongs or horns in their hands, which from time to time they struck, or from which they blew long wailing blasts, and then demanded alms from the passers by in the boldest manner. Altogether it was a strange and bewildering scene.

As we stood gazing there, a band of pilgrims, in a state of almost complete nudity, came up from the river. Their long, dishevelled locks hung wildly round their haggard faces, and they looked as if they had travelled far and suffered great privations. In consequence of a vow, one of them had neither washed nor combed his hair for years, and it now fell like disgusting knotted cables over his shoulders. Slowly each drew nigh, with hands devoutly clasped, and holding between the palms a sprig of the sacred *tulasi* plant, which was consecrated to the god. They muttered prayers as they came up, and paused when they reached the front of the temple. Here they threw themselves down at full length in the sacred dust, which rose in clouds; then over and over they rolled, all the way to the opposite side, a distance of many yards, just stopping for a moment to worship as they passed the main entrance. A priest now raised them up, one by one, when they proceeded to walk round about the temple, with hands still devoutly raised and clasped as before. The whole of this they performed three times, after which they bathed in the river, and were then admitted into the presence of their god. Not one of the pilgrims seemed to notice us, so absorbed did they appear in their devotions.

Now another larger group arrived on the scene; and this time I felt so sick at heart, that I could not bear to watch longer. Not only men, but along with them women and young girls, threw themselves grovelling in the dust, and rolled over and over as the others had done, to the opposite side. Still sadder, and yet more painful spectacles than these are always to be witnessed during the weeks of the great annual festival. The infatuated worshippers carry fire in the palms of their hands for a given distance, and others thrust wires through their cheeks and limbs. Some will make the circuit of the temple, in every position of uneasiness and torture, till they not unfrequently sink fainting on the ground. There is a man wearing a heavy iron collar, the bars of which project so far that he cannot possibly recline night or day. We spoke to one of these, and he told us that he had begun to make an idol, and not having money to finish it, he had vowed that he would wear this iron collar until he should raise the necessary funds. See! yonder is a father proudly initiating his little child in its first act of idol worship. It can scarcely walk steadily alone as yet, but he cheers it on, and teaches it to clasp its dimpled hands, and prostrate itself on the ground many times. The little one looks up as it passes, with a ready smile on its innocent face as it meets the pitying eye of the Missionary standing there. He turns away to hide his emotion.

Oh, how congenial it is to the human heart to *do* some great thing in order to inherit eternal life! How hard it is for a Hindu to lay all his penances, fastings, pilgrimages, and costly offerings down as absolutely worthless at the foot of the Cross! How difficult for him to accept by simple faith in the Name that from his childhood he has been taught to hate, the free, unmerited gift of pardon and heaven! *It is hard*, and Jesus knows it. Oh! why are so few prayers offered up in Christian homes for these benighted ones? Why are such poor, such grudging responses made to their plaintive call for more light?

The sun was by this time blazing fiercely overhead, so we retired to a sort of pavilion just in front of the temple, where we could still see all that was going on. Here for an hour and a half my husband reasoned with a large crowd who gathered round us, on the folly and sin of idol worship. Some stopped their ears, and beating their mouths said, 'Such words ought not to be listened to for a single moment,' and walked away. But many remained, while the Missionary with a full heart told them of the simple and only way to true rest, happiness, and heaven. A school of prettily dressed little Hindu boys now came marching up, and stopped on seeing us. Eager to display his lore, the master made them chant Sanscrit *slokas* in praise of the gods. They did so, taking parts very cleverly. He next insisted on making his pupils go through a kind of gymnastic dance, singing all the while. They were bright, intelligent little fellows and did their very best to exhibit their prowess.

By this time we were exceedingly hot and weary, so we repaired to our conveyance in the grove by the river, to seek a little quiet. But there we were again quickly surrounded by an eager crowd asking for books. Group followed group, and as we could not refuse a kind word of advice as we gave out the tracts, we were ere long so utterly exhausted, that we were compelled to tell the people that we must rest awhile, so they reluctantly left us. We had now leisure to survey the scene around us. Up and down, all along the side of the Capila, little groups of pilgrims were seated under the spreading trees. Some were reclining, evidently quite fatigued by their penances and devotions. Others had just returned from the temple in garments dripping wet, and were now having their heads shaven. At short intervals, devotees with fixed gaze and folded hands paced solemnly along, muttering their prayers and prostrating themselves. Then a corpse was carried past us on a litter to the water's edge, where at a short distance from our conveyance we watched it burning.

As a further variety to the strange scene, our horse, never very amiable, had become incensed to the last degree by the impertinence of a bullock, which dared to taste his bundle of grass. With a great bound he broke loose, and forthwith commenced a desperate chase after all the cattle grazing near us. This episode created no little confusion and alarm among the pilgrims, but a number of them kindly lent their aid in capturing our irreverent steed. So excited had he become, that we did not secure him for nearly an hour, and till he had plunged into the river. On our way home that evening, we found all the *choultries*, or wayside rest houses, crowded with natives returning from Mysore, where they had been celebrating the great Dasari feast. They had kindled little fires all around in the open air, and now sat talking in groups, while they prepared their supper of pepper-water or curry and rice, by the light of the stars.

From beginning to end, that day was one never to be forgotten by us. We had seen so many illustrations of the power which Hinduism still exerts over the millions of its deluded votaries, that our hearts were sad indeed. Perhaps never before did we realise more vividly the magnitude of the work yet to be done ere India shall own but one God.

Some years later, while sojourning in the lovely island of Tasmania, one of the Australian colonies, in quest of health to enable us to return to our beloved work in Mysore, a touching incident one day threw quiet, peaceful Hobart Town into a state of intense excitement. The news quickly spread that a boy, twelve years of age, had been lost on Mount Wellington from the previous day. This noble mountain, which could be distinctly seen from most parts of the town and its suburbs, was the loftiest point of a fine range in the immediate neighbourhood. It was surrounded by a belt of low jungle, familiarly known there as 'scrub.' The mayor immediately convened a meeting of the inhabitants, many of whom left their business and came flocking together. Three different search parties were organised, composed of volunteers who understood the windings and dangerous places about the mountain. Some who could not go, readily offered money to meet expenses, while others promised to supply suitable provisions. The first party were to start within a few hours, the second, by torch-light, about midnight, and the third at day-break. They promised to prosecute the search till the boy was discovered, dead or alive. Little else was talked about in the town, and many eyes watched the beacon fires kindled along the hill-side as the darkness deepened. About noon the next day the quick report of cannon announced to the people that the lost was found alive; and all rejoiced in the common joy, as if the lad had been a friend or brother.

LOST ON MOUNT WELLINGTON.

'HE is lost upon the mountain!'
Fast and far the tidings ran,
To the mansion and the cottage,
On they passed from man to man.

'He is lost!' and many a mother,
Bending o'er her sleepers fair,
Shuddering thought upon the mountain,
And the lonely wanderer there.

'He is lost!' and strong men hied them
To the rescue one and all;
Asking not, 'Is he my brother?'
Waiting not for friendship's call.

'T is enough a life 's in danger,
Only one, *some* mother's child,
And the city's heart is throbbing
With a tumult strange and wild.

'We will go,' said some, and hastened;
'We will give' said some, and gave;
Each man quickly knew his talent,
Did what best he could to save.

Heard you not that wail of anguish?
Sleepers, up for Jesus' sake!
'T is no time for idle slumbers;
Hark again that call, Awake!

Lo! on black and dismal mountains,
Hung with ever deepening night,
Full of pitfalls, snares, and mazes,
With no track, no guide, no light,

Mighty nations hasten onwards
  To the ever yawning tomb,
With no ray of dawn celestial
  Breaking through the starless gloom.

Women, men, and little children,
  Whom your Saviour died to buy,
Priceless souls that may be rescued,
  Dare you leave them thus to die ?

Strive, oh strive to realise it ;
  Did you but believe it true,
You would agonise and wrestle,
  You would flee to save them too.

Men of God, awake to duty !
  For their blood will He demand,
In the solemn day of reckoning,
  At His slumbering Church's hand.

CHAPTER XI.

A SANCTUARY FOR THE CHRISTIANS' GOD.

UNDER a tree in the streets of Mysore the Missionary has taken his stand, in the freshness of early morning. The *pettah* has just woke up to busy life. Money-changers are adjusting their scales, arranging their testing-stones and little heaps of coin. Merchants are already seated cross-legged in the midst of their stores—cloth, grain, oil, or sweetmeats, as they may chance to be—quite ready for customers. Multitudes pass to and fro, casting a curious or a careless glance at the preacher and the crowd that is now gathering round him. Women with great piles of grass which they cut for the horses nicely poised upon their heads, or long bundles of *cholum* stalks for cattle, move slowly along; while many others are carrying baskets full of cow dung, which the natives of India use freely in cleansing their houses, as well as to burn, after it has been dried in the sun. One or two of these draw near to the outside of the listening throng, attracted by the earnest tones of the Missionary. Many of his audience know him well, and some of them seem to feel the power of his burning words. The preacher's heart is enlarged this morning, as he points his dark-eyed hearers to the Crucified, and he yearns, with unspeakable longing, to hear the cry, 'What must we do to be saved?'

Suddenly a mocking voice rings through the crowd: 'Show us your God, and we will believe you.'

Then turning to the men around him, the Brahman

THE NATIVE CHAPEL, MYSORE.

sneeringly exclaims, 'The *padre sahib* has neither a god nor a temple to show us, why listen to him?'

The laugh is now turned against the Missionary, and with a look of ineffable contempt this emissary of Satan turns on his heel, and walks away, followed by many others, who but a few moments before seemed almost persuaded to be Christians.

Sorely does the disappointed servant of Christ feel this taunt, for there is some reason for it. Around him on either side his eye rests on many a proud *pagoda,* the gilded *kalashas* of which flash as the morning sunbeams play upon them. The rich sculpturing which adorns these shrines, and still more the gold and gems inside with which their gods are decked, tell how much a Hindu will lavish in the service of an abominable idol. There, just behind the southern wing of the palace, stands the temple of Kristnaswàmy, built by his highness the Rajah at a cost, it is said, of £40,000. In addition to this, a grand *mantapa,* or porch, of stone has since been added, which cost £5,000 more. The door facing the idol is covered with gold, and the most costly jewels adorn the god. Nearly two hundred Brahmans and eight dancing girls are maintained there, to conduct the temple service.

There, too, the Missionary can see the domes and graceful minarets of many a Mohamedan mosque. Nor is there wanting the church adorned by the cross, where the Romanist burns incense, sprinkles holy water, and performs his devotions with many an imposing rite. But the little room within the Mission compound, in which the humble group of native Christians met every Sabbath to worship God, was so unlike any of these, and so inconveniently small, that it was no wonder the heathen failed to recognise it as the temple of the Christians' God. Oh how earnestly we longed to build a house worthy of Jehovah! but we had not the money, and we would not dishonour His name by incurring a heavy debt.

One Sabbath morning an unwonted blessing rested on all during the service. Our hearts seemed to burn within us, and my husband knew, that day, that God would ere long grant us our desire. So immediately on our return home, we consecrated, on our knees, a small offering with which to assist in laying the foundation stone. One kind friend after another added a brick to the building, and we went on collecting in cheerful faith.

The jubilee anniversary of our Missionary Society, was celebrated in October, 1863. We invited all our native Christians to rejoice with us, and to partake of coffee, &c. As I moved hither and thither before the time, arranging cakes, fruit, and flowers upon the tables, John, our oldest native member, entered, and, with a *salaam*, sat down. He was a sepoy in the Rajah's service, and his entire income was some nine or ten shillings a month. He was a venerable looking old man, with thin, silvery locks, and a wrinkled but radiant face. He was deeply attached to the Missionaries. Once when I was prostrated with Indian fever, John walked a long way to see me. Finding that I was too ill to get up, he entreated that he might be allowed just for a moment to see his '*tai*' (mother), for so he always called me. On entering the room, he immediately prostrated himself on the floor, and offered up such a prayer for my restoration to health, as did me more good, I believe, than all the medicine I was taking.

Among the eager listeners in our little native church every Sabbath day, John was always conspicuous for his earnest attention. Bending forward to catch every word that fell from the lips of the preacher, the aged saint seemed to hear each time as for eternity.

Now, with all the simplicity of a little child, the dear old man had come an hour too soon, in haste to anticipate the joy of our jubilee gathering. For a while he sat silently watching me, then coming forward, he said,—

'*Tai* (mother), you take a great deal of trouble to make us happy, now I want to tell you something that will make your heart glad.'

'Well John, what is it?' I asked of my grey-haired son.

'I have brought an offering with me which I want to give you now, to help to build a house for our God,' replied the good old Christian, at the same time placing in my hand a parcel of silver rupees.

Much moved by his noble generosity, I remonstrated, for I knew well that he could only afford to bring such a gift by exercising the most painful self-denial. But John had already counted the cost. He loved his God better than he loved himself; and he rejoiced to endure privation for a while, that he might enjoy the blessed privilege of assisting to raise a house for Jehovah's glory.

District Meeting time came, and all our Christians eagerly awaited my husband's return from Bangalore, to learn the decision of the meeting respecting our new chapel. But a very large one was just then in course of erection for the English congregation there, so it was deemed well to defer ours till that should be completed. As soon as the Missionary arrived, old John presented himself at the Mission house, and asked, his face all quivering with emotion,—

'*Ayàh*, what of God's house?'

'Oh, John, they tell us we must wait.' Here he was interrupted by a great burst of weeping from the aged Christian.

'But we *shall* have one ere long,' continued my husband.

'Oh, but I had hoped that these eyes should have been permitted to see it before I die,' cried John.

And it was a sorrow to us all, but we still went on collecting what we could; and during our absence in England, the funds grew rapidly under the warm advocacy of the Rev. J. H. Cummings. On our return to Mysore in 1869, Mr. Hutcheon received the sanction of District Meeting at once to proceed with the work. The promise of an iron roof, and a suitable plan had been obtained while in London; so our way was made plain, and the building was immediately begun.

It is Christmas morning. The mists yet linger around the brow of Chamundi, and the birds have scarcely commenced their matin songs, when we are suddenly roused from our slumbers by the booming of cannon. What can it mean? Ah! we remember now, for we have heard it before. It was the custom of the old heathen Rajah of Mysore to cause a royal salute to be fired, at daybreak, every Christmas morning, in honour of the birthday of the Lord Jesus. Soon we are all astir, for this ushers in a busy and eventful day. At 7 a.m. all our native Christians have assembled in the Mission compound; and now they march across to the site of our new chapel, which just overlooks the main entrance to the *pettah*, singing hymns as they go. Fervent prayers are offered, and then, with great joy, we lay the first twelve bricks of the foundation. Four months later, under a noble pavilion, kindly lent for the occasion, the foundation stone was formally laid by Colonel Mallison, guardian to His Highness the young Rajah of Mysore, in the presence of a large concourse of both English and native spectators.

But to return to Christmas morning. After laying the bricks, we adjourned to the little old chapel, where a short service was held, and six babies—kept waiting for this great occasion—were baptized. By invitation of our people, we next proceeded to the large hall of our English Institution, where they had provided a most sumptuous breakfast for us. This was certainly a new phase of things, and afforded very pleasing evidence of the growing strength and self-reliance of our native Church. The extent of the preparations they had made took us quite by surprise. A table laden with the best of English and native fare was spread for the Missionaries, while our Christians sat ranged along the hall, the men on one side, and the women and children on the other. Curry and rice, with fruit and sweetmeats, were served out to all; then followed many short speeches, in simple but heartfelt words of love and encouragement.

In the evening, we held the first native Missionary meeting in the city of Mysore. Our people were in raptures with it, and laboured to express their delight. '*Ayàh*,' said one, 'that was not an ordinary happiness, it was a *mahà santosha*—a great joy.'

All our Christians watched the progress of the new building with the deepest interest. But only those who have had a similar experience can know all the hard yet happy toil that devolved on the Missionary, ere the chapel was completed. In turn, he had to be purchaser and measurer of wood, sand, *chunam*, and bricks. He had next to be master builder, and truly his patience was often sorely tried ere some pretty little gothic window was nicely moulded, or other detail of the plan was successfully carried out, for the native workmen had never erected a building of the kind before. Then the design for the end window of stained glass, as well as for the reading desk and communion rail, had each to be sketched at the Mission house. The cushions, too, had all to be made under our own eye. But no one thought of grudging the labour, or esteemed it anything but a great privilege to be allowed to lend a helping hand in this blessed work. Even the heathen looked on with considerable curiosity and interest. Some of their remarks pleased us very much. '*Ayàh*, that is a temple worthy of Para Brahma, the God of gods,' said one. 'Well, your temple is just like your religion, very pure and spotless,' said another.

At length our joy was consummated when, after a week of special prayer, our holy and beautiful house was opened for public worship. It was a glorious morning. A flood of sunlight streaming through the coloured window, fell in showers of rainbow hue on the chaste mosaic floor and stainless walls. These were composed of polished *chunam*, which gleamed in its purity like fair white marble. Our native Christians, wearing bright new cloths, purchased for the occasion, sat with radiant faces in the front ranks. Behind, sat many fine looking, high caste youths, students at our English Institution, and others, the very flower of

Mysore. When all rose, and we took possession of the chapel in the King's name, by our first anthem, 'Crown Him Lord of all,' I could only weep for very gladness. We have often tasted happiness, both before and since that hour, but a purer joy than that which then filled our hearts to over-flowing, we can never know, till earth has faded, and the beatific Vision bursts upon our raptured gaze.

Yet there was one worshipper absent, whom we would fain have seen in our midst on that glad Sabbath morn. Hidden from our eye, yet perchance not far away, dear old John had gone to worship God in His 'house not made with hands, eternal in the heavens.' He died, but had not seen the sight for which he so willingly endured privation, as well as prayed and longed. Ere he passed into the higher temple, he gave his entire possessions, sixteen rupees, or £1 12s., with the small mud-walled cottage in which he lived and died, 'to help to raise a house to the Christians' God.' Once to royal David in his cedar galleries came the blessed approval of the King of kings, when he so ardently desired to build a house worthy of His great name. 'Thou didst well in that it was in thine heart.' Can we doubt, then, that to the aged Christian in his lowly mud tenement, came a plaudit as gracious, since he 'of his penury' had cast into God's treasury, 'all the living which he had'?

'Look unto Me, and be ye saved, all the ends of the earth: for I am God, and there is none else' (Isaiah xlv. 22), was the inspiring text of that first Canarese service. It was no wonder that the Missionary was drawn out beyond himself. In the afternoon, our beloved native Minister, Rev. Abijah Samuel, preached with great unction. In the evening the first English service was conducted by the Rev. T. Hodson, the respected Chairman of the District. God's presence was felt throughout the whole of that memorable Sabbath in an unusual degree.

It seemed as if our God had just permitted us to return to India to see this work, on which our hearts had so long been set, accomplished; for a few months later my health so completely failed, that the only hope of recovery lay in our at once seeking a more salubrious clime. Yet, ere we departed, perhaps to return no more, our gracious Lord gave us the crowning proof of His truth and faithfulness, by bringing in the last of the group of women, for whose conversion we had prayed *during ten years.*

When our first converts were baptized, their mothers wives, and sisters were their most bitter persecutors. They hid their clothes, so that they could not attend the means of grace; they followed them about everywhere, and by their constant tears and abuse greatly tried the stability of the young disciples. We strove by various means to reach them, but apparently without success. We tried to induce them to come to a Bible reading or mothers' meeting, that they might hear for themselves the truths which had wrought such a wonderful change in the lives of their sons and husbands, but all in vain. One would come for a week or two, then, being laughed at and mocked by her heathen neighbours, no entreaty would win her back to the meeting. So our three colleagues and ourselves agreed to make these women the subjects of special daily prayer, till they too should be brought to a knowledge of the truth as it is in Jesus. Six years passed, and we were about to return to England for change in 1866, when the first answer came. A fine young woman, the most intelligent of the group for whose salvation we had prayed so long, decided for Christ. She was named Parinjoti, her baby boy being baptized at the same time.

That was indeed a great joy; and during our absence one after another was gathered into the Church, till now that we were about to say farewell to the land of our adoption, our faithful God said, Amen, to many prayers, in bringing in the last of that once persecuting little band. She was the aged mother of one of our most promising converts, and hers was the first adult baptism in our new sanctuary. It was a touching sight to see her kneel with her fine, manly son by her side, and to remember how much he had endured for the sake of the blessed Master, whom at the eleventh hour she had learned to love. Three months after this she was seized with mortal sickness, and died in great peace, trusting alone in the merits of the Lord Jesus.

Would that during these ten years there had been on our part no slackness in believing prayer, no fainting of heart, because the blessing tarried! Oh, how God's condescension and goodness rebuked our languid faith and feeble prayers! Surely if we have not, it is because we ask not, or because we ask amiss; for a faithful, covenant-keeping God, is the Lord Jehovah.

CHAPTER XII.

PEEPS INTO HINDU HOMES.

'YOU must show me favour, by coming to teach the ladies of my house some good customs,' said a wealthy and influential Brahman to me one day, as we sat chatting together. I was much pleased as well as surprised by his request, for we had always regarded him as a Hindu of the most rigid type. He had spent large sums of money in building a *choultry*, or wayside rest house, and in other equally meritorious works. His father, many years before, had undertaken a pilgrimage all the way to the holy city Benares, in the far north, and brought back to his family a priceless treasure in the form of a quantity of water from the sacred river Ganges. He had thereby secured, in his estimation, sufficient merit, not only to avail for himself, but for his household also.

The old man died, but the precious water remained as his legacy in the family. At length his widow, the aged grandmother, resolved to increase and crown the good works of her husband and children by prevailing on them all to set out on pilgrimage to Ramnad, in the extreme south of India. Here they would worship in its famous temple, and conclude by pouring the holy Ganges water, which they had kept so sacredly, upon its celebrated god. The ceaseless importunities of the old lady prevailed; and the whole family, herself included, went on the journey a distance of five hundred miles. At the end of several months they returned very much poorer in purse and person, but rich indeed they believed in fame and merit. So altered was the eldest son, the hope of the family, through fever caught by the way, that I failed to recognise him on his arrival.

This youth, with his younger brother, had for some years been studying successfully in our English Institution; and for a considerable time before receiving the invitation to visit them, the father had himself become a frequent visitor at the Mission house. When my husband happened to be engaged, he would sometimes come and talk with me as I sat at work; and his prejudices gradually began to tone down. Some have argued, that our Missionaries would have greater influence with the natives of India if they resided among them, and conformed more fully to their usages, giving up the little refinements and comforts which tend to throw such a charm around our British firesides. But to me it seems evident that our bright and attractive Christian homes, in contrast with their own dark and cheerless ones, must form a more irresistible argument.

Hindus are quick observers, and as our rooms, though neat and comfortable, were never so fine as to exclude our native friends, we soon found that nothing escaped their attention. In these days *zenana* schools were unheard of in the city of Mysore; but I had long wished to obtain access to some Hindu homes, that I might have a chance of conversing with the native ladies, whom we never meet outside. This I could only gain by special invitation, so I most gladly complied with the request of our Brahman friend. He named an early day for our visit, asking my husband to accompany me.

His house, inside the fort, was a large and substantial one, built of stone, and two stories high. The large hall, to which we were conducted with much ceremony, opened at the farther end into the inner court. The ladies at once ran off with me to this side, while the gentlemen, seated on chairs, sat talking at the other. My readers will remember that native houses in India are almost, if not altogether, destitute of furniture. The Hindus feel no need of it. The ground, covered by a mat or rug, answers equally for chair or bedstead. It forms the table also, which requires neither plate nor crockery. Leaves neatly stitched together suffice for plates and dishes; a brass *jumboo,* or vessel, serves for all drinking purposes, and this they do not allow their lips to touch, while the fingers supply the place of knives, forks, and spoons. Together husband and wife, brother and sister may never sit down to enjoy a social meal. The wife's invariable duty is first to wait upon her lord; and then, his wants being attended to, she may retire and dine at a respectful distance, with the other females of the household.

But to return to our visit. The ladies were by no means so bashful as I expected on a first interview. Being quite away from the gentlemen, they seemed determined to use their opportunity by asking me a host of questions.

'Have you any children?'

'Why do you wear your hair in that way?'

'Why is your skin so much fairer than ours?'

'Why is your dress black? and why do you wear so few jewels?'

'How do you spend your time?'

'Can you cook and sew, as well as read and write?'

'How many meals a day have you?'

'Do your servants give you what they like, or do you give orders about everything?'

As I tried to satisfy their curiosity on these weighty subjects, the gesticulations, merriment, and comments were very amusing. Still, I pitied them more. Scarcely one of all their questions was worthy of a creature possessing an immortal soul. Little, indeed, did their aspirations seem to rise above the mere animal. Ere we left them we spoke as much as in a first interview we dared to do, of the blessedness of that religion which makes us to differ.

There were, I think, twelve or fifteen ladies seated on the ground around me during this visit. Some of them were young, fair, and beautiful. The lower caste females in India are very inferior in appearance, and much darker in colour than those of the higher. Such however, are almost the only ones ever seen in this country, being native *ayahs* or nurses. I have often wished that we could bring home a good specimen of a Brahman gentleman, lady, and child; I feel sure they would bespeak far deeper interest for their people than has ever yet been felt in Britain.

Yes; the ladies and children of India are often strikingly beautiful. There is the large, lustrous, dark eye, softened by its long, silken fringes. The features are regular and delicately moulded, with the well-formed head and the slight, graceful figure. The hair, black as the raven's wing, is glossy and abundant. It is generally worn by the higher classes in one long braid or plait behind, fastened by gold ornaments;

but by the lower orders it is invariably arranged in a sort of chignon, inclining to the left side. The cushion used in forming this is composed of the flowers and buds of the fragrant jasmine. Their complexion varies from a bright brown to a shade scarcely darker than the complexion of an English brunette. Such, however, are seldom to be seen outside the walls of the *zenana*. If the jealousy of their husbands permits them to go abroad at all, it is in a closely curtained palanquin, or coach with closed venetian shutters.

The dress of a Hindu female, which is most graceful, consists of a long robe, or, rather, scarf, called the *sheerè*. It is composed of bright coloured gauze, silk, muslin, or cotton, according to the rank and taste of the wearer; or it may be of snowy white, with a broad border of gold, or of some gay tint. It is woven in one piece, about nine yards in length, by a yard and quarter in width. The mode of wearing it is this. One end is wrapped two or three times around the person in the form of a skirt, descending from waist to ankle. Several folds are neatly arranged and secured at the left side. The remaining end is then passed across the chest, over the right shoulder, and caught under the left arm. But in the presence of strangers, or on going abroad, this is thrown gracefully over the head, and even the face, as a veil. The only other article of dress worn by a native lady is the tiny *kuppasa*. This is a small, tight-fitting bodice, tied in a knot across the bosom. It has very short sleeves, so narrow that the arm can with difficulty be squeezed into it. Silk or other pretty showy material is generally used for this.

The jewels of a Hindu lady are magnificent, and

often represent the greater part of the family fortune. A large, round ornament of gold adorns the back of her head, while her long, glossy plait is bound with another. Her ears, up and down, sparkle with the choicest gems. Some of these form exquisite little flowers, and bear the closest inspection. The rings or pendants in the lower part of the ear, are so very large and massive as to leave a most unsightly hole when removed. The nose has a small and costly jewel inserted at one side, and frequently a large ring or fringe of pearls droops over the upper lip, forming to European eyes a rather questionable ornament. The neck, arms, wrists, and fingers sparkle with chains and bands of gold; while the waist, ankles, and toes are encircled by bands and fringes of silver. The Hindus say, that the person who degrades gold by wearing it on the lower members of the body, will live to know its value by the want of it.

I may explain here why so many ladies should be found in one *zenana*. This is owing to the strength of the patriarchal system in India. Not only parents and grandparents, unmarried children and married sons, but also a number of more distant relatives, will continue without scruple to reside under one roof, and claim support, just so long as the purse of the householder will warrant their doing so. Polygamy, though frequent, especially where the first wife is childless, is by no means universally practised. It prevails, however, to a sad extent at native courts.

Now, will the reader accompany me to another Hindu home, if we may designate these cheerless dwellings by that dear and familiar name? The family whom we are about to visit was one of some note, its head being the brother of a former very distinguished prime minister of the Rajah of Mysore. From their position in society we expected to see a handsome house; but in this we were disappointed, for we were guided to a large, two story high dwelling, built for the most part of mud and sun-burnt bricks. All the gentlemen of the household met us in the outer court, and after shaking hands led us along a dark, narrow lobby into a small hall. Its furniture consisted of a carpet, four armchairs, and a long earthen seat, built by the side of the wall, which, covered with a rug, answered for a couch. Here the gentlemen pointed us to chairs, and themselves sat down on the seat beside us. They talked intelligently on a variety of subjects, several of them speaking English well.

A very tiny baby girl, nine months old, but scarcely larger than a big doll, was now brought in and placed in my arms. Children of even Brahman families in India run about their homes without a single vestige of clothing up to the age of five or six. In the villages they go out and play in this state all day long. The tiny lady I now held formed no exception to this rule as far as clothing went. But from the crown of her little black head to her small toes she was literally covered with gold, jewels, and rings and bells of silver. I confess I never felt more awkward in my life; for much as I love babies, I scarcely knew how to handle one like that. Should you, my young reader?

We were next informed that the master of the house, a very aged man, would pay his respects to us. We were requested, as a particular favour, not to touch him, as he had just bathed; and being a very holy man, the touch of even our garments would necessitate his bathing again. This seemed scarcely complimentary, but we knew enough of caste tyranny to understand it all, and we were not ready to take offence, so we promised to be most careful. A very decrepit old gentleman was now brought in, with every mark of the deepest respect. A chair was placed for him at a safe distance from us, on which he sat down and eyed us closely. Being satisfied thus far, he addressed my husband in Canarese, and began to tell him the names of the many great men he had known in his day. He, along with most of the gentlemen, soon took leave, and the ladies of the house were introduced.

Carefully avoiding the Missionaries, they shook hands with me, seating themselves by my side. They were richly and tastefully attired, and wore a profusion of valuable jewels. The mistress of the house then addressed me in a carefully prepared little Canarese speech. She assured me that her house was that day honoured in a remarkable degree by the visit of 'such a great goddess.' I found it by no means easy gracefully to acknowledge a compliment so rare. At least, I had scarcely then been long enough in India to feel quite comfortable after such an oration. But I told her how glad I was to make the acquaintance of herself and family.

I was much pleased with the grace and modest bearing of several of the ladies; but there was one among them over whom my heart yearned with inexpressible tenderness. She was a young girl, some fifteen years of age, decidedly more beautiful than either of her happier sisters. She wore no jewel, and the dim red cloth, the shaven head, and the sad, dejected mien at once told us that she was a widow. I noticed that when the other ladies came forward and shook hands, she avoided me, and like an inferior being went and sat down humbly behind them. My sympathy was fully awakened, and holding out my hand I spoke a few loving words to her. But looking at me with a groan, and a world of sadness in her fine, dark eye, she only said:

'*Nanage bahala avamàna.*' (To me there is great dishonour.)

To favoured Israel God's command was, 'Ye shall not afflict any widow, or fatherless child. If thou afflict them in any wise, and they cry at all unto Me, I will surely hear their cry.' (Exodus xxii. 22, 23.) And there, as in Christian Britain, such have always enjoyed a special share of tenderness and sympathy. Why? Because the nature and name of the God we profess to serve is *love*, and the glorious badge by which the followers of the Lord Jesus are to be distinguished is also love. It is fitting, then, that we, like our great Master, should delight to own the peculiar claim of the broken-hearted, the bruised, and the helpless ones. But poor India bows down to gods of jealousy, cruelty, and lust. What wonder then is it, that her sons and daughters have never learnt to weep with and for those who groan under the heaviest of all bereavements! To become the bird of ill omen, the cause of all the calamities that befall the family, and to be made the domestic drudge, is the sad lot of the young Hindu widow.

The iniquity of this cruel treatment is greatly aggravated by the fact, that the young creature thus execrated has herself had no voice whatever in the choice of her husband. She was betrothed when but a little child, of most likely from four to seven years of age, to one of whom she knows nothing, and perhaps has never even seen. Her parents may have given their child for gold to the highest bidder, and she may never yet have lived with him. It matters not; from the moment he dies she is a widow, for betrothal is just as binding upon her as the second ceremony, or marriage, can be.

But, thank God! a few gleams of heaven's own light have begun to break into the darkness of the *zenana*. The once awfully common crime of female infanticide, even in Rajputana, where it was estimated that twenty thousand female infants were at one time annually murdered, is almost, if not altogether, suppressed by the powerful interference of the British government. No longer does the widow burn on the pyre of her dead husband as in the olden days; and one other step towards the day of her redemption has been taken, in the passing of that humane act which renders the re-marriage of widows in India lawful. Soon after it came into force, two little girls were rescued from the cruel fate that otherwise would certainly have awaited them in Midnapore. The first child bride was betrothed when five years of age, and her husband died the same year; the other was betrothed, and became a widow when only four years old! The parents, gladly availing themselves of the new act, had their little innocent children betrothed a second time.

Once, through the courtesy of a Brahman friend, we were invited to be present at a native family festival. This was held on March 28th, being the Hindu

New Year's Day. It is the custom on this evening, for the bridegrooms elect to be entertained at the house of their future fathers-in-law; and in southern India, where *zenana* seclusion is not enforced with such extreme rigour as in Bengal, even the female members are permitted to be present on this festive day. We were ushered into a large apartment, which was brightly illuminated by many white and coloured lamps. At the door, musicians with lutes and *tom-toms* did their best to entertain the company. One large group of Vydeekaru, or sacred Brahmans, occupied the centre of the room in front of us, and another of Loukeekaru, or secular Brahmans, sat on the floor at our left. All the ladies of the household, with their female relatives, were closely packed together in a corner on our extreme right; and from time to time at the command of the master, '*Hardi*' (Sing), they at once struck up a native lyric. But the chief objects of general interest were two little brides, aged eight and eleven years respectively, with their boy bridegrooms.

One of these was the daughter of our host, a beautiful child, who had already been betrothed for four years. They occupied a sort of raised daïs at the end of the hall, and husband and wife were seated together on cushions, an honour these little girls would never enjoy after their marriage. A lovely little bride, the elder of the two was, as she sat there sparkling with jewels, looking just like a wax figure. She wore a crimson and yellow *sheerè* of rich silk. Across the top of her head was fastened an elegant band of garnets set in gold, and a jewelled pendant drooped over her forehead. Two round golden ornaments clasped her hair behind, while another glittering band extended all down the long plait in which her black, glossy hair was arranged. Exquisitely wrought gems, such as I have already described elsewhere, adorned her nose, ears, neck, arms, wrists, and fingers, forming a display quite dazzling. With all the half bashful consciousness of a young native beauty, she from time to time placed betel-nut and leaf into the mouth of her future lord, but never lifting her eyes towards him. The other little bride did the same to her boy husband. This compliment they condescended once or twice to return during the evening. The girls then rose, and respectfully approaching their lords, they threw a garland of flowers around their necks. The husbands then with great dignity garlanded their brides, keeping their seats as they did so.

It was altogether a singular exhibition, saddened to us by the knowledge that the lad to whom that pretty little creature had already been united was a very wicked youth. So violent was his temper, that on the slightest provocation he threatened to jump into a deep well, and so commit suicide. This he had actually attempted once, but was rescued in time. And yet, knowing all this, and conscious that should he carry out his favourite threat that sweet child would at once become a widow, nothing could be done. Already she was bound to him by an indissoluble tie.

During this visit we were strikingly reminded of a New Testament parable, by a point in Hindu etiquette. The entertainment of the evening was long delayed, because several of the expected guests had not arrived. A servant was sent literally 'to say to them that were bidden, Come, for all things are now ready.' How many Bible scenes and usages have we seen exactly reproduced in India!

There are many peculiarities in Hindu etiquette which a Missionary does well carefully to notice, if he would avoid needlessly giving offence, for natives are most sensitive on these points. 'What a fine little fellow!' you say pleasantly to a native mother, as she passes you with her chubby baby boy on her side. But she receives your well-meant civility with no smile of fond, maternal pride, as any happy mother in our own land would do. No; with a start and a look of unaffected dismay on her countenance, she hurries off to the nearest astrologer to procure a charm, which she immediately fastens on her child. Your admiration has directed the attention of 'the evil eye' to her golden boy, and without this precaution she believes that in all probability he would soon begin to pine away and die.

You make some kind and polite remarks to the mistress of the house you are visiting, and wait for her reply. But she looks confused, and moves away to a distance, leaving her visitor to feel most uncomfortable. While you sit wondering how you could possibly have offended your native friend, a feeling of relief returns with the recollection that you have forgotten one of the laws of Hindu etiquette, which forbids a wife to speak to strangers in the presence of her husband or mother-in-law.

It is a hot Indian day, and your tailor feels it to be so, as he sits cross-legged on the bamboo mat in the verandah, patiently stitching the most dainty little garments. He has laid his turban on one side for a few minutes, to wipe the perspiration from his shaven head and brow. But he hears 'Missus' coming, and quick as thought the turban is put on again. Ramaswammy knows good breeding too well to speak to a lady with his head uncovered. It would be an equally unpardonable offence against native ideas of politeness, for a Hindu to enter your house with his shoes on his feet. These are left outside on all occasions, whether on entering school, chapel, or dwelling. One gentleman may not make kind inquiries about the health of his friend's wife, for this would be regarded as a serious offence against the rules of propriety.

Our Mysore Canarese *munshi,* an intelligent and in many respects superior man, had just been married for the second time to a timid girlish bride, in whom I felt interested. One day, I ventured to say so him, 'I do hope, *munshi,* that you love your pretty young wife and treat her very kindly.' He looked disconcerted and replied:

'O ma'am, it would never do for me to say that.'

'Why not?' I asked, though I guessed what his answer would be.

'There would be no more peace in store for me, ma'am, if my wife only suspected that I loved her,' was his reply.

Yes; a Hindu may freely show his love for his father, his brother, or his friend, but let him beware how he manifests this to the wife of his bosom. The *shastras* declare that 'falsehood, cruelty, bewitchery, folly, covetousness, impurity, and unmercifulness, are woman's inseparable faults.' Again, 'Woman's sin is greater than that of man.' 'Her sin cannot be removed by the atonement which destroys his.' It is also enjoined 'Let not women be much loved, let them have only that degree of affection which is necessary; let the fulness of affection be reserved for brothers, and other similar connections.'

Think on this, ye daughters of England, whose most valued possession, next to the smile of Jesus, is the undisputed love of a true and manly heart. What would these homes of yours, either in prospect or in possession be, if that were denied? Yet without this blessed talisman, which makes duty pleasure, labour easy, and even suffering seem light, the young Hindu wife is compelled to render the most servile homage and unquestioning obedience to every command or caprice of him she calls husband. He may be ignorant, wicked, old, and childish; it matters not, he is to her instead of God. 'To wash his feet, and drink the water,' is to the wife a 'sacred ablution.' 'The husband is her god, and priest, and religion, and its services; wherefore, abandoning everything else, she ought chiefly to worship her husband.'

At his pleasure the wife is closely immured in the *zenana*, with no pleasant variety of occupation or recreation to beguile the monotony of the weary hours. She has no knowledge of music or of the fine arts; she cannot even sew. Why should she learn, since that is 'tailor's business'? Read or write she cannot; for knowledge is power, and the less of that she wields the better for all parties. Her husband probably can read, but he would consider it infinitely beneath his dignity to do so for her edification. Besides, the few books of the household would do little indeed towards elevating her. They are interspersed with such stories of the doings of gods and men, as makes modesty hide her head.

That Hindu ladies have all the latent capabilities

for receiving education and refinement of the highest kind there can exist no doubt. The little girls in our principal schools, who on entering seem to have no distinct idea about anything, begin in a short time to manifest great sprightliness and intelligence. They have simply never been taught to think or act for themselves; but the mind once roused to activity, there is no difficulty in teaching them anything. I was much pleased on one occasion to receive a wax flower made for me by a Hindu lady, in token of her friendship. Some pretty and ingenious toys made of beads and wire were also sent by her for our little girl, and where *zenana* schools have been established, fancy work is always eagerly learnt. Most Hindu wives take considerable pride and pleasure, also, in being reckoned skilful in mixing and blending the various condiments used in preparing their curries. Though all Brahmans are vegetarians, and loathe even the name of animal food, yet there is greater variety in the apparently unvarying routine of curry and rice than many persons imagine. A gentleman of good social position and family, once asked permission to send us specimens of the different native dishes made in his house. I gladly consented; and the next day a large tray was sent, containing tiny, brightly polished, brass vessels, filled with curries of many kinds. Beside them were neatly stitched little dishes made of leaves, and in these was rice prepared in a great variety of ways. Next day and the following came pickles and chutneys of many sorts, with native cakes, sweet dishes, and confections, till we begged our generous friend to send no more. To Europeans these curries are almost uneatable, being so excessively hot and so saturated with ghee, as even their sweets are; but little native children, as well as adults, eat them with the greatest relish.

The approach of a festival or a wedding in the family is hailed with delight by the occupants of the *zenana*, as creating a welcome bustle and diversion. For with the exception of preparing the two simple meals a day, and waiting on her husband, the Hindu lady has little or no occupation, beyond fondling her children, braiding her hair, arranging her jewels, and eagerly listening to any idle gossip or foolish story that may be brought to her. The companion, confidante, and helpmate of her husband she may not hope to be; for she is a *woman*, and according to their *shastras* that means, as already quoted, an inferior being, naturally so prone to all evil, that sternness, severity, and to be kept at a distance are the only wise modes of treatment. Such are some, and but some of women's wrongs in India. Still, we rejoice to believe that not a few Hindus are better than their harsh, unjust creed. One intelligent Brahman gentleman spoke to us of his buried wife with tearful eyes, and his voice faltered with emotion as he said, 'In all our *Agràhara* her equal is not left.'

Yes; even in India, woman has a power and an influence peculiarly her own, which no oppression or neglect can altogether take from her. But who can wonder, and who shall blame, if that power be frequently used there for evil rather than for good? Idolatry has no devotees more blind and superstitious than are to be found in the *zenana*. After threats, cruelty, and bribes have alike failed to lure the young convert from his allegiance to the Lord Jesus, how often have the ceaseless tears, entreaties, and importunities of a mother prevailed!

But a brighter, better day has begun to dawn upon India. Already in some blessed instances God has permitted us to see the transforming power of Divine grace on Hindu women. I once asked of one, very simple, and very ignorant of all but saving faith in Christ;

'Do you know that you have obtained a new heart, and a title to heaven?'

She looked up at me with a smile, and a tear stood in her eye as she answered;

'Yes, *amma*, surely I done get it.'

'But how can you tell?' I questioned, though her life had told us more plainly than words that she was indeed a new creature in Christ Jesus.

She paused for a moment, and then replied;

'First time, when I begin to pray, *amma*, only my *lips* telling prayers; but now same like *my heart hungry to pray*.'

Once, in a season of deep trial, she became my humble comforter and faithful friend. As she sat on the floor beside me, her face buried in her hands, I heard her murmuring softly as if unconscious of all around. I listened, and my heart grew strong again as I heard her talking to the Lord Jesus. In the simplest words, just as a little child would tell its griefs to one it fondly loved and trusted, she was telling her Master and mine all about our sorrow; and she urged Him to come quickly to help us, as only one who was on the most intimate terms could do. The Lord whom she served heard, and was neither 'slow to hear nor impotent to save.'

We have seen, too, God's grace changing the persecuting Hindu mother into the zealous Christian worker, the helper of her son's faith, which once she sought to destroy. And it has been our privilege to watch her as she came up to the margin of the dark river, and fearlessly stepped into the surging waters, while her heathen sister 'lingers shivering on the brink, and fears to launch away.' That Name which alone is music to the dying ear is on her lip; that Arm upon which a fainting head can only rest is around and underneath her; and softly whispering, '*Yèsuvè, Yèsuvè*,' she passes through death more than conqueror.

But God is Himself arising to undertake the cause of the daughters of India. Doors that but a few short years ago seemed hopelessly bolted and guarded against every effort of the Christian teacher, or Missionary's wife, are now being thrown open in every direction. We view the rapid change with amazement, and joyfully recognise that the unseen hand which all silently has drawn the bars and bolts aside is the Lord's. Oh, if His followers are but ready now to do their duty, if they will at once enter in where Providence has so signally prepared the way, who shall estimate or foretell all the blessed results that may quickly follow! How soon may the *zenana* be transformed from a dull and cheerless prison house into a happy Christian home? May not the hand of our faith grasp the day, not in the far distance, but as drawing nigh, when the Hindu woman shall recognise in the Lord Jesus her glorious emancipator, the true vindicator of her rights, and her loving, almighty Friend?

But one solemn question rises here. *Are* Christians in this land of Bibles and of happy homes doing or even striving to do their duty to India? Linked as it is to our own country by the finger of Providence, can we refuse, without blood-guiltiness, to send the light of life into these dark and loveless dwellings? I confess that when in Mysore I struggled, often single-handed and alone, to do something for heathen women, amid discouragements of every kind, I could bear up in hope of the reaping by-and-by. But when about to leave India, with shattered health and ebbing strength, we saw wide doors for usefulness inviting us on every side, and no one to enter in at them, then my heart grew faint indeed, and I felt as if I could only sit down and weep in very helplessness.

Once, on the Nielgherries, it was our happiness to be invited to meet three devoted sisters, English ladies of education and fortune, who, constrained by the love of Christ, had come to consecrate their lives, talents, and property to this one grand object of raising their sisters in the far East. Oh! why are such noble examples so few and far between? Why comes that oft repeated and pitiful cry echoing across the wave, 'Send us help speedily! oh, send us men and women of the right stamp'? Why is the work of two or three men often thrown upon one solitary Missionary, who bravely stands in the breach, because he will rather die at his post than give up ground gained at such cost, so long as he can hold it? Is it not because Christian fathers and mothers fail to own in the fullest sense the claims of Jesus, when He calls their best and most gifted sons and daughters to this difficult but glorious work? Even the home Churches too often refuse to spare their choicest men for these distant and trying fields. And yet, it was to rescue the *one* sheep that was lost that the good Shepherd left the ninety and nine, whose needs were so much less urgent.

Perhaps never did we realise so fully the true value of life and its momentous issues, as we did while standing beside the two lonely but well-known graves in the island of St. Helena. That of the great Napoleon, who to secure his own ambitious ends, to immortalise his name, and to bind a matchless wreath of laurels around his brow, scrupled not to sacrifice the peace and welfare of vast nations, and to shed the hearts' blood of their bravest and noblest sons. But life and life's dream were ended; and even ere it closed, these costly and ill won laurels had already begun to fade. There, too, lay the blessed dust of sweet Sarah Judson, of America and Burmah; a heroine in a truer, higher sense. She, treading in the footprints of her humble Lord, and seeking not her own glory but His, rejoiced to spend and to be spent in leading the daughters of Burmah to know and love her Saviour and theirs. On one side of the marble obelisk which a loving Church has raised to her memory is the command of Jesus, 'Go ye into all the world, and preach the Gospel to every creature'; and on the other, the simple but grand encomium, 'She hath done what she could.' Will the Master repeat this, dear reader, as He utters your name and mine, in the day when He shall come to take account of our stewardship?

ST. HELENA'S TWO GRAVES.

VISITED BY US ON OUR HOMEWARD VOYAGE, IN 1874.

STRONG in thy proud, embattled cliffs,
Lone isle, we leave thee now,
The white surf moaning at thy feet,
The stars upon thy brow.

When labouring earth, convulsed, was rent
With strong internal throes,
Thy dark volcanic peaks and knolls
From ocean's depths arose.

A narrow empire for a king,
Whose hand had sought to clasp
The destinies of half a world,
Within its iron grasp!

How must that regal bird have pined,
Shut in such massive cage!
How did he beat his crippled wings
In vain and helpless rage!

Those crested, bounding billows, too,
Rejoicing all around,
To him were but stern sentinels,
Guards of his prison ground.

Oh, could he, like the sea-bird, soar
On pinions gladly free,
How swiftly had he skimmed the wave
To France and liberty!

'T is past; and though thy own loved France
At last the debt has paid;
Though there thy discrowned head once more
In regal pomp be laid:

Methinks, within that sculptur'd pile,
Thy dreamless rest will be
No sweeter than in yon lone isle,
Beneath the willow tree.

But, St. Helena, thou hast urned
More dear, more cherished dust,
One of heaven's choicest gems was given
To thy most sacred trust.

Sweet Sarah Judson sleepeth too
Beneath the banyan shade,
From Burman, and New England shores
Afar her tomb is made.

But, oh, on that triumphant morn
When thrones and crowns are given,
Not always to earth's royalty
But to the heirs of heaven;

Dear sister, from thine island bed
By faith I see thee rise,
To join a glad expectant throng
From Burmah in the skies.

Wilt *thou*, O emperor, awake
As joyful from thy rest,
To stand approved, acknowledged, crowned
Among that concourse blest?

Stern island fastness, fare thee well,
Dim and far distant now,
Thou standest proudly and alone,
The stars upon thy brow.

Standard and Popular Works,

PUBLISHED AT THE

WESLEYAN CONFERENCE OFFICE.

THEOLOGICAL.

Arthur (W.) The Tongue of Fire; or, the True Power of Christianity. By the Rev. W. ARTHUR, M.A. Royal 32mo. Price 1s.; Gilt edges, 1s. 4d.

Dunn (L. R.) The Mission of the Spirit; or, the Office and Work of the Comforter in Human Redemption. By the Rev. LEWIS R. DUNN, Minister of the Methodist Episcopal Church, U.S. Edited by the Rev. JOSEPH BUSH. Crown 8vo. Price 2s.

Edmondson (J.) Sermons on Important Subjects; with an Introduction by the Rev. T. JACKSON. Two Vols. Crown 8vo. Price 6s.

Fletcher (J.) An Appeal to Matter of Fact and Common Sense; or, a Rational Demonstration of Man's Corrupt and Lost Estate. By the Rev. JOHN FLETCHER. 12mo. Price 2s.

Fletcher (J.) Five Checks to Antinomianism. By the Rev. JOHN FLETCHER. 12mo. Price 4s. 6d.

Fletcher (J.) The Works of the Rev. John Fletcher; with his Life, by the Rev. JOSEPH BENSON. Complete in Nine Volumes. 12mo. Price £1 11s. 6d.

Geden (J. D.) Didsbury Sermons: Being Fifteen Dis-courses preached in the Wesleyan College Chapel, Didsbury. By JOHN DURY GEDEN, Tutor in Hebrew and Classics. 8vo. Price 7s.

Gregory (B.) The Holy Catholic Church, the Communion of Saints: Being the FERNLEY LECTURE for 1873. With Notes, and Essays on The History of Christian Fellowship, and on the Origin of 'High Church' and 'Broad Church' Theories. By the Rev. B. GREGORY. 8vo. 4s. 6d.

Gregory (J. R.) An Examination of the Doctrines of Con-ditional Immortality and Universalism. By the Rev. J. ROBINSON GREGORY. Crown 8vo. Price 3s. 6d.

10—78

Hannah (J.) Introductory Lectures on the Study of Christian Theology: with Outlines of Lectures on the Doctrines of Christianity. By the late Rev. JOHN HANNAH, D.D.; to which is prefixed a Memoir of Dr. Hannah, by the Rev. W. B. POPE, D.D. Crown 8vo. Price 3s. 6d.

Horbery (M.) An Enquiry into the Scripture Doctrine concerning the Duration of Future Punishment. By MATTHEW HORBERY, B.D. Reprinted from the Edition of 1744.

Jackson (T.) The Duties of Christianity; theoretically and practically considered. By the Rev. THOMAS JACKSON. Second Edition. Crown 8vo. Price 4s.

Jackson (T.) The Institutions of Christianity, exhibited in their Scriptural Character and Practical Bearing. By the Rev. THOMAS JACKSON. Crown 8vo. Price 5s.

Jackson (T.) The Providence of God, viewed in the Light of Holy Scripture. By the Rev. THOMAS JACKSON. New Edition with Improvements. Crown 8vo. Price 4s.

Jackson (T.) The Christian armed against Infidelity. Treatises in Defence of Divine Revelation. Foolscap 8vo. Price 2s.

M'Afee (D.) The Pillar and Ground of the Truth. Twelve Sermons on the Fundamental Truths of Christianity. By the Rev. DANIEL M'AFEE. With a Preface, by the Rev. WILLIAM ARTHUR, M.A. Crown 8vo. With Portrait. Price 6s.

Pope (W. B.) A Compendium of Theology: Biblical, Dogmatic, Historical. By the Rev. WILLIAM B. POPE, D.D., Theological Tutor, Didsbury College. Second Edition. 3 Vols., 8vo. Price £1 11s. 6d.

Pope (W. B.) Sermons, Addresses, and Charges delivered during his year of office. By the Rev. W. B. POPE, D.D., late President of the Wesleyan Methodist Conference. 8vo. Price 8s. 6d.

Pope (W. B.) The Person of Christ: Dogmatic, Scrip-tural, Historical. The Fernley Lecture for 1871. With two additional Essays on the Biblical and Ecclesiastical Development of the Doctrine, and Illustrative Notes. By the Rev. W. B. POPE, D.D., Theological Tutor, Didsbury College. 8vo. Price 7s.

Pope (W. B.) The Prayers of St. Paul. Being an Analysis and Exposition of the Devotional Portion of the Apostle's Writings. By the Rev. W. B. POPE, D.D. 8vo. Price 7s.

Prest (C.) The Witness of the Holy Spirit. By the Rev. CHARLES PREST. Third Edition. Crown 8vo., cloth, red edges. Price 3s.

Randles (M.) For Ever! An Essay on Eternal Punish-ment. By the Rev. MARSHALL RANDLES. Third Edition. Crown 8vo. Price 5s.

Robinson (E. J.) How to Pray and What to Pray For. An Exposition of the Lord's Prayer and Christ's Introductory Sayings. By the Rev. EDWARD JEWITT ROBINSON. Crown 8vo. Price 5s.

Robinson (E. J.) The Caravan and the Temple, and Songs of the Pilgrims. Psalms cxx.—cxxxiv. By the Rev. E. J. ROBINSON. Crown 8vo. Price 3s. 6d.

Robinson (E. J.) The Mother of Jesus not the Papal Mary. By the Rev. E. J. ROBINSON. Crown 8vo. Price 6s.

Treffry (R.) Inquiry into the Doctrine of the Eternal Sonship of our Lord Jesus Christ. By the Rev. RICHARD TREFFRY, Jun. Crown 8vo. Price 6s.

Waddy (S. D.) Sermons. By the late Rev. SAMUEL D. WADDY, D.D. Crown 8vo. Price 4s.

Watson (R.) Sermons and Sketches of Sermons. By the Rev. RICHARD WATSON.

Three Volumes, demy 8vo. Price 18s.
Three Volumes, post 8vo. Price 10s. 6d.

Watson (R.) Theological Institutes; or, a View of the Evidences, Doctrines, Morals, and Institutions of Christianity. By the Rev. RICHARD WATSON. Four Volumes, royal 18mo. Price 14s.

Watson (R.) The Works of the Rev. Richard Watson. With his Memoirs, by the Rev. THOMAS JACKSON.

Thirteen Volumes, demy 8vo. Price £3 18s.
Thirteen Volumes, post 8vo. Price £2 5s. 6d.

Wesley (J.) Fifty-three Sermons by the Rev. John WESLEY, M.A. These Sermons, and Mr. Wesley's Notes on the New Testament, constitute the Standard Doctrines of the Methodist Connexion. Crown 8vo. Price 3s. 6d.

Wesley (J.) Sermons on Several Occasions. By the Rev. JOHN WESLEY, M.A. Complete edition, containing One Hundred and Forty-one Sermons, and a Life of the Author by the Rev. JOHN BEECHAM, D.D. Three Vols., crown 8vo. Price 7s. 6d.

Fine Edition, three Vols., crown 8vo. Price 10s. 6d.
Library Edition, three Vols., demy 8vo. Price 18s.

Wesley (J.) The Prose Works of the Rev. John Wesley, M.A. Edited by the Rev. THOMAS JACKSON. This Edition contains all the Latest Corrections of the Author; and includes the Life of Mr. Wesley by the Rev. JOHN BEECHAM, D.D.

Library Edition, Fourteen Volumes, demy 8vo. Price £4 4s.
Cheap Edition, Fourteen Volumes, post 8vo. Price £2 2s.

Wiseman (L. H.) Christ in the Wilderness; or, Practical Views of our Lord's Temptation. By the Rev. LUKE H. WISEMAN, M.A. Crown 8vo. Price 3s. 6d.

Wood (T.) The Doctrines of Annihilation and Universalism viewed in the Light of Reason, Analogy, and Revelation. By the Rev. THOMAS WOOD. Crown 8vo. Price 2s.

COMMENTARIES, DICTIONARIES, &c., ILLUSTRATIVE OF THE HOLY SCRIPTURES.

Aids to Daily Meditation: being Practical Reflections and Observations on a Passage of Scripture for each Day in the Year. Crown 8vo., cloth. Price 3s. 6d.

The Holy Bible: with Notes, Critical, Explanatory, and Practical. By the Rev. JOSEPH BENSON. With Maps and a Portrait of the Author. Six Volumes, Imperial 8vo., cloth, red edges. Price £3 3s.

A Biblical and Theological Dictionary: Illustrative of the Old and New Testaments. By the Rev. JOHN FARRAR. With Four Maps and Ninety-six Engravings. Crown 8vo. Price 3s. 6d.

An Ecclesiastical Dictionary: Explanatory of the History, Antiquities, Heresies, Sects, and Religious Denominations of the Christian Church. By the Rev. JOHN FARRAR. Crown 8vo. Price 5s.

Helps to the Study of the Bible, containing Analytical Notes, and Summaries of the several books; Historical, Chronological, and Geographical Tables; List of Animals, Birds, Reptiles, Plants, &c., found in Scripture; Tables of Weights, Measures, and Time; Words Obsolete or Ambiguous; together with a new Index to the Bible, Cruden's Concordance, a Dictionary of Scripture Proper Names, and a series of Maps. Foolscap 8vo. Price 2s.

The Proper Names of the Bible; their Orthography, Pronunciation, and Signification. With a brief Account of the Principal Persons, and a Description of the principal Places. By the Rev. JOHN FARRAR. 18mo. Price 1s. 6d.

A Commentary on the Old and New Testament; contain-ing copious Notes, Theological, Historical, and Critical; with Improvements and Reflections. By the Rev. JOSEPH SUTCLIFFE, M.A. Imperial 8vo., cloth, marbled edges. Price 12s. 6d.

The Synoptical Dictionary of Scripture Parallels and References; being an Index of the Texts of Scripture Classified; forming a Methodical Summary of the Principles, Doctrines, Precepts, and Facts of Scripture. 8vo. Price 2s. 6d.

A Biblical and Theological Dictionary: Explanatory of the History, Manners, and Customs of the Jews, and neighbouring Nations. With an Account of the most remarkable Places mentioned in Sacred Scripture; an Exposition of the principal Doctrines of Christianity; and Notices of Jewish and Christian Sects and Heresies. By the Rev. RICHARD WATSON. Royal 8vo., cloth, red edges. Price 12s. 6d.

An Exposition of the Gospels of St. Matthew and St. Mark, and of some other detached parts of Scripture. By the Rev. RICHARD WATSON. Demy 8vo., Price 6s.; 12mo., Price 3s. 6d.

The New Testament, with Explanatory Notes. By the Rev. JOHN WESLEY. With the Author's last Corrections.
Pocket Edition. 18mo. Price 2s.
Large-Type Edition. 8vo. Price 4s.
Library Edition, fine paper. Demy 8vo. Price 6s.

An Exposition of St. Paul's Epistle to the Romans. By the Rev. HENRY W. WILLIAMS, D.D. Crown 8vo. Price 6s.

An Exposition of the Epistle to the Hebrews. By the Rev. HENRY W. WILLIAMS, D.D. Crown 8vo. Price 6s.

The Incarnate Son of God; or, the History of the Life and Ministry of the Redeemer; arranged, generally, according to Greswell's Harmony of the Gospels. By the Rev. HENRY W. WILLIAMS, D.D. Crown 8vo. Price 4s.

Scripture compared with Scripture. A Plan for Daily Bible Reading throughout the Year. Arranged by E. G. C. Price 4d. Limp cloth, gilt edges, 6d.

BIOGRAPHICAL.

Asbury (Francis), The Pioneer Bishop: Life and Times of. By W. P. STRICKLAND. Royal 32mo. Price 1s.; Gilt edges, 1s. 4d.

Alpine Missionary (The); or, the Life of J. L. Rostan, Missionary Pastor in France, Switzerland, and the Channel Isles. By the Rev. MATTHEW LELIEVRE. Translated from the French Edition, by the Rev. A. J. FRENCH, B.A. With a Portrait. Crown 8vo. Price 3s. 6d.

Bamford (J.) The Disciple among the Poor: Memorials of Mr. John Bamford, of Shardlow. By his Son, the Rev. JOHN M. BAMFORD. Crown 8vo. Price 3s. With Photographic Portrait, 3s. 6d.

Bramwell (W.) The Christian Minister in Earnest. A Memoir of the Rev. William Bramwell; containing Extracts from his Correspondence, and a Delineation of his Personal and Ministerial Character. By the Rev. THOMAS HARRIS. With a Portrait. Royal 18mo., gilt edges, Price 3s.
Cheap Edition. Royal 32mo. Price 1s.

Bumby (J. H.) The Life of the Rev. John H. Bumby. With a brief History of the Progress of the Wesleyan Mission in New Zealand. By the Rev. ALFRED BARRETT. With a Portrait. 12mo. Price 3s.

Bunting (William M.), Memorials of. Being Selections from his Sermons, Letters, and Poems. Edited by the Rev. G. STRINGER ROWE. With a Biographical Introduction by THOMAS PERCIVAL BUNTING. Crown 8vo. Price 3s. 6d.

Carvosso (W.) Memoirs of William Carvosso. Written by himself, and edited by his Son. With a Portrait. Royal 18mo. Gilt edges. Price 2s. 6d. Cheap Edition. Royal 32mo. Price 1s.

Clarke (A.) The Life of Dr. Adam Clarke. By the Rev. Dr. ETHERIDGE. With a Portrait. Post 8vo. Price 3s. 6d.
Cheap Edition. Royal 32mo. Price 1s. 6d.

Coke (T.) The Life of Thomas Coke. By the Rev. Dr. ETHERIDGE. With a Portrait. Post 8vo. Price 3s. 6d.
Cheap Edition. Royal 32mo. Price 1s. 6d.

Dixon (J.) The Life of James Dixon, D.D., Wesleyan Minister. Written by his Son, RICHARD WATSON DIXON, M.A., Minor Canon in Carlisle Cathedral Church. With three Portraits of Dr. DIXON, and a Vignette of his Birthplace. Crown 8vo. Price 7s. 6d.

Dixon (T.) The Earnest Methodist. A Memoir of the late Mr. Thomas Dixon, of Grantham. By his Nephew, the Rev. JOSEPH DIXON. Foolscap 8vo. With Portrait. Price 2s.

Entwisle (J.) Memoir of the Rev. Joseph Entwisle: with copious Extracts from his Journals and Correspondence, and Occasional Notices of Contemporary Events in the History of Methodism. By his Son. With a Portrait. Crown 8vo. Price 3s.

Father Reeves, the Methodist Class Leader. By EDWARD CORDEROY. 18mo. Price 1s.

Fletcher (J.) The Life of the Rev. John Fletcher. By the Rev. JOSEPH BENSON. With a Portrait. 12mo. Price 3s. 6d.
Cheap Edition. Royal 32mo. Price 1s.

Fletcher (Mrs.) The Life of Mrs. Fletcher. By the Rev. HENRY MOORE. With a Portrait. Crown 8vo. Price 3s. 6d.
Cheap Edition. Royal 32mo. Price 1s.

George (E.) Memoirs of Elizabeth George. By the Rev. HENRY J. PIGGOTT, B.A. With a Portrait. Crown 8vo. Price 2s. 6d.

Grimshaw (W.), Incumbent of Haworth. By the Rev. R. SPENCE HARDY. With a Portrait. Crown 8vo. Price 3s.

Hare (R. H.) The Ministry and Character of Robert Henry Hare, Wesleyan Minister. By JOHN MIDDLETON HARE, his Brother. Crown 8vo. With Portrait. Price 6s.

Hessel (Eliza.) True Womanhood; or, Memorials of Miss Eliza Hessel. By the Rev. JOSHUA PRIESTLEY. Crown 8vo. With Portrait. Price 2s. 6d.; gilt edges, 3s.

Hunt (J.) The Life of John Hunt, Missionary to the Cannibals in Fiji. By the Rev. GEORGE STRINGER ROWE. Foolscap 8vo. With Portrait. Price 2s. 6d.; limp cloth, 1s. 6d.

Jackson (T.) Lives of Early Methodist Preachers. Chiefly written by themselves. Edited, with an Introductory Essay, by the Rev. THOMAS JACKSON.

Library Edition, Six Vols. Crown 8vo. Price 15s.
Cheap Edition, Six Vols. Foolscap 8vo. Price 9s.

Jackson (T.) Recollections of My Own Life and Times. By THOMAS JACKSON. Edited by the Rev. B. FRANKLAND, B.A. With an Introduction and Postscript by G. OSBORN, D.D. With a Portrait. Crown 8vo. Price 5s.

M'Owan (P.) A Man of God; or, Providence and Grace Exemplified in a Memoir of the Rev. Peter M'Owan. Compiled chiefly from his Letters and Papers. By the Rev. JOHN M'OWAN. Edited by G. OSBORN, D.D. Crown 8vo. Price 5s.

Maxwell (Lady). The Life of Darcy Lady Maxwell. By the Rev. WILLIAM ATHERTON. With Selections from her Diary and Correspondence. Crown 8vo. Price 3s. 6d.

Miller (W. E.) Life of the Rev. W. E. Miller. By the Rev. Dr. DIXON. Foolscap 8vo. Price 2s.; limp cloth, 1s. 6d.

Nelson (J.) The Journal of Mr. John Nelson. Royal 18mo. Price 1s. 6d.

Cheap Edition. Royal 32mo. Price 10d.

Newton (R.) The Life of the Rev. Robert Newton, D.D. By the Rev. THOMAS JACKSON. With a Portrait. Crown 8vo. Price 2s. 6d.

Cheap Edition. Royal 32mo. Price 1s. 6d.

Ouseley (Gideon.) The Life of Gideon Ouseley. By the Rev. WILLIAM ARTHUR, M.A. Seventh thousand. Crown 8vo. With Portrait. 3s. 6d. Tree-marbled calf, gilt edges. Price 10s. 6d.

Richardson (C.) The Peasant Preacher: Memoir of Mr. Charles Richardson. By the Rev. J. E. COULSON. Royal 32mo. Price 1s.; Gilt edges, 1s. 4d.

Rogers (Mrs.) The Experience and Spiritual Letters of Mrs. Hester Ann Rogers. 18mo. Gilt edges. Price 1s. 6d.

Cheap Edition. Royal 32mo. Price 10d.

Rogers (Mrs.) The Experience, Letters, and Journal of Mrs. Hester Ann Rogers. Royal 18mo. Gilt edges. Price 3s. 6d.

Shaw (Barnabas.) The Story of his Life and Labours in South Africa. By the Rev. WILLIAM MOISTER. Crown 8vo. Portrait and Illustrations. Price 3s. 6d.

Shaw (W.) Memorials of the Life and Labours of the Rev. WILLIAM SHAW, late General Superintendent of the Wesleyan Missions in South Africa. By his oldest surviving Friend. Crown 8vo. With Portrait. Price 6s. 6d. Cheap Edition. Crown 8vo. Price 2s. 6d.

Shaw (Mrs.) Long Life and Peace: Memorials of Mrs. ELIZABETH SHAW, of St. Austell. By the Rev. ROBERT C. BARRATT. Foolscap 8vo. Price 3s.

Shillington (T. A.) Christian Thoroughness: A Memorial Sketch of THOMAS AVERELL SHILLINGTON, J.P., of Portadown. By the Rev. JOHN DWYER, Author of 'Christian Work for Gentle Hands,' &c. Crown 8vo. Price 3s.

Shrewsbury (J. B.) Christ Glorified in the Life, Experi-ence, and Character of Joseph B. Shrewsbury (late Medical Student, and Wesleyan Local Preacher, of Bradford, Yorkshire). Written by his Father. Royal 32mo. Price 1s.; Gilt edges, 1s. 4d.

Smith (J.) Memoirs of the Life, Character, and Labours of the Rev. John Smith. By the Rev. R. TREFFRY, Jun. With an Introductory Essay by the Rev. Dr. DIXON. Royal 18mo. Gilt edges. Price 3s.
Cheap Edition, without the Introductory Essay. Price 1s.

Stoner (D.) Memoirs of the Rev. David Stoner. By the Rev. Dr. HANNAH and Mr. WILLIAM DAWSON. With a Portrait. Royal 18mo. Gilt edges. Price 2s. 6d. Cheap Edition. Royal 32mo. Price 1s.

Taylor (M. C.) Memoir of the Rev. Michael C. Taylor. With Extracts from his Correspondence. By the Rev. B. HELLIER. Crown 8vo. Price 3s. 6d.

Threlfall (W.) Memorials of the Rev. W. Threlfall. By the Rev. SAMUEL BROADBENT. 18mo. With Portrait. Price 1s. 6d.

Toase (W.) Memorials of the Rev. William Toase. Compiled by a Friend. With an Introduction by the Rev. WILLIAM ARTHUR, M.A. Crown 8vo. Price 3s. 6d.

Treffry (R.) Memoirs of the Rev. R. Treffry, Jun. With Select Remains, consisting of Sketches of Sermons, Essays, and Poetry. By his Father, the Rev. RICHARD TREFFRY. With a Portrait. 12mo. Price 4s. 6d.

Tucker (Mrs. J.) Memoir of Mrs. Jane Tucker, wife of the Rev. Charles Tucker, some time Missionary to Haabai and Tonga. By Mrs. G. F. WHITE. Edited by the Rev. H. W. WILLIAMS, D.D. Crown 8vo. Price 2s. 6d.

Turner, James; or, how to Reach the Masses. By E. M'HARDIE. Crown 8vo. Price 3s.

Waddy (S. D.) The Life of the Rev. Samuel D. Waddy, D.D. By his Youngest Daughter. Crown 8vo., with Two Portraits. Price 5s.

Watson (R.) Memoirs of the Life and Writings of the Rev. Richard Watson. By the Rev. THOMAS JACKSON. With a Portrait. Royal 18mo. Price 3s. 6d. 8vo. Price 6s.

Wesley (C.) The Life of the Rev. Charles Wesley. Comprising a Review of his Poetry; Sketches of the Rise and Progress of Methodism; with Notices of Contemporary Events and Characters. By the Rev. THOMAS JACKSON. With a Portrait. Crown 8vo. Price 3s. 6d.

Wesley (C.) The Journal of the Rev. Charles Wesley. With Selections from his Correspondence and Poetry, and an Introduction by the Rev. THOMAS JACKSON. Two Vols. Royal 18mo. Price 7s.

Wesley (J.) The Life of the Rev. John Wesley. By the Rev. RICHARD WATSON. With a Portrait. Crown 8vo. Price 3s. 6d.
Cheap Edition. Royal 32mo. Price 1s. 4d.

Wesley (J.) His Life and his Work. By the Rev. M. LELIEVRE. Translated by the Rev. A. J. FRENCH. With a Portrait. Crown 8vo. Price 3s.

Wesley (J.) The Living Wesley, as he was in his Youth and in his Prime. By the Rev. JAMES H. RIGG, D.D., Principal of the Wesleyan Training College, Westminster. Crown 8vo. Price 3s.

Wesley (J.) The Father of Methodism: A Life of the Rev. JOHN WESLEY, A.M. By Mrs. COSSLETT. Second Edition, enlarged. Foolscap 8vo. Profusely Illustrated. Price 1s. 6d.

Wesley (J.) The Journals of the Rev. John Wesley. Four Vols. 12mo. Price 10s.

West (F. A.) Memorials of the Rev. Francis A. West. Being a Selection from his Sermons and Lectures. With a Biographical Sketch by one of his Sons, and Personal Recollections by the Rev. B. GREGORY. Crown 8vo. Price 4s.

Wharton (H.) The Story of the Life and Missionary Labours of the Rev. Henry Wharton in the West Indies, the Gold Coast, and Ashanti. By the Rev. W. MOISTER. Crown 8vo. With Portrait and Illustrations. Price 3s. 6d.

Wood (J.) The Life of the Rev. Joseph Wood. With Extracts from his Diary. By the Rev. H. W. WILLIAMS. With a Portrait. Crown 8vo. Price 3s.

Wesley's (Rev. John and Charles) Poetical Works: A New and Complete Edition. Reprinted from the Originals, with the last corrections of the Authors; together with the Poems of CHARLES WESLEY not before published. Collected and Arranged by the Rev. GEORGE OSBORN, D.D. Thirteen Volumes. Crown 8vo. Price £3 18s.

The Methodist Family Library.

ROYAL 32mo.	Cloth, Plain edges.	Cloth, Gilt edges.
1. Nelson's, Mr. John, Journal . . .	0 10	1 0
2. Rogers, Mrs. H. A., Experience and Letters of	0 10	1 0
3. Martin's, Mrs., Life. By Rev. B. FIELD .	0 10	1 0
4. Told, Mr. Silas, Life of	0 10	1 0
5. Carvosso, Mr. William, Memoir of . .	1 0	1 4
6. Fletcher's, Mrs. Mary, Life . . .	1 0	1 4
7. Fletcher's, Rev. John, Life . . .	1 0	1 4
8. Prayer: Secret, Social, and Extempore. By Rev. R. TREFFRY, Sen., and Rev. JOSEPH WOOD	1 0	1 4
9. Stoner's, Rev. D., Memoirs . . .	1 0	1 4
10. Smith's, Rev. John, Life. By Rev. R. TREFFRY, Jun.	1 0	1 4
11. Entire Sanctification Attainable in This Life; being John Wesley's 'Plain Account of Christian Perfection;' and John Fletcher's 'Practical Application of the Doctrine to Various Classes of Christians'	1 0	1 4
12. Asbury, Bishop, Life and Times of . .	1 0	1 4
13. Shrewsbury's, Joseph B., (Medical Student) Memoir	1 0	1 4
14. Bramwell's, Rev. W., Life and Letters. By Rev. T. HARRIS	1 0	1 4
15. Wesley's, Rev. John, A.M., Life. By Rev. R. WATSON	1 4	1 9
16. Clarke's, Dr. Adam, Life. By Dr. ETHERIDGE	1 6	2 0
17. Coke's, Dr. Thomas, Life. By Dr. ETHERIDGE	1 6	2 0
18. Newton's, Dr. Robert, Life. By Rev. T. JACKSON	1 6	2 0
19. The Tongue of Fire; or, the True Power of Christianity. By Rev. W. ARTHUR, M.A.	1 0	1 4
20. The Peasant Preacher; Memoir of Mr. C. Richardson. By Rev. J. E. COULSON .	1 0	1 4

Illustrated Books for School and Home.

PRICE FIVE SHILLINGS.

The History of Methodism, from its Origin to the Centenary Year. By ABEL STEVENS, LL.D. In three Volumes, Crown 8vo., with Portraits. Price 5s. each.

Romance without Fiction; or, Sketches from the Portfolio of an Old Missionary. By the Rev. HENRY BLEBY, Author of the 'Death Struggles of Slavery,' &c., &c. Crown 8vo. Eight Page Illustrations.

PRICE FOUR SHILLINGS.

Zoology of the Bible. By HARLAND COULTAS. With Preface by the Rev. W. F. MOULTON, D.D. Imperial 16mo. 126 Illustrations.

Missionary Anecdotes, Sketches, Facts, and Incidents, Relating to the state of the Heathen and the Effects of the Gospel in various parts of the World. By the Rev. WILLIAM MOISTER. Crown 8vo. Eight Page Illustrations.

Northern Lights; or, Pen and Pencil Sketches of Nineteen Modern Scottish Worthies. By the Rev. J. MARRAT. Crown 8vo. Portraits and Illustrations.

PRICE THREE SHILLINGS AND SIXPENCE.

Chronicles of Capstan Cabin; or, the Children's Hour. By J. JACKSON WRAY. Imperial 16mo. Twenty-eight Illustrations.

The Life of Gideon Ouseley. By the Rev. WILLIAM ARTHUR, M.A. Seventh Thousand. Crown 8vo. With Portrait.

Missionary Stories, Narratives, Scenes, and Incidents, Illustrative of the Providence and Grace of God in Connection with the Propagation of the Gospel in Heathen Lands. By the Rev. W. MOISTER. Crown 8vo. Eight Page Illustrations.

Sunshine in the Kitchen; or, Chapters for Maid Servants By the Rev. B. SMITH, Author of 'Climbing,' etc. Fourth Thousand. Crown 8vo. Numerous Illustrations.

BY THE SAME AUTHOR.

Way-Marks: Placed by Royal Authority on the King's Highway. Being One Hundred Scripture Proverbs, Enforced and Illustrated.

Gems Reset; or, the Wesleyan Catechisms Illustrated by Imagery and Narrative.

PRICE TWO SHILLINGS AND SIXPENCE.

A Pledge that Redeemed Itself. By SARSON, Author of 'Blind Olive,' etc. Crown 8vo. Numerous Illustrations. Cloth, gilt edges.

Glimpses of India and Mission Life. By Mrs. HUTCHEON. Crown 8vo. Eight Page Illustrations. Cloth, gilt edges.

The Story of a Peninsular Veteran: Sergeant in the 43rd Light Infantry during the Peninsular War. Crown 8vo. Numerous Illustrations.

Rays from the Sun of Righteousness. By the Rev. RICHARD NEWTON, D.D. Crown 8vo. Eleven page Illustrations. Cloth extra. Gilt edges.

In the Tropics; or, Scenes and Incidents of West Indian Life. By the Rev. JABEZ MARRAT. Crown 8vo., with Illustrations, &c.

Climbing: A Manual for the Young who Desire to Rise in Both Worlds. By the Rev. BENJAMIN SMITH. Crown 8vo. Sixth Edition. Revised and Enlarged.

MARK GUY PEARSE'S WORKS.

Six Volumes, Crown 8vo., Cloth, Gilt Edges. Price 2s. 6d. each.

1.—**Daniel Quorm, and his Religious Notions.** FIRST SERIES. Forty-second Thousand.

2.—**Daniel Quorm, and his Religious Notions.** SECOND SERIES.

3.—**Sermons for Children.** Eleventh Thousand.

4.—**Mister Horn and His Friends; or, Givers and Giving.** Thirteenth Thousand.

5.—**Short Stories; and other Papers.**

6.—**'Good Will:' a Collection of Christmas Stories.**

The Stolen Children; A Narrative compiled from Authentic Sources, by the Rev. HENRY BLEBY, Author of 'Death Struggles of Slavery.' Foolscap 8vo., gilt edges, with Illustrations.

Our Visit to Rome, with Notes by the Way. By the Rev. JOHN RHODES. Royal 16mo. Forty-five Illustrations.

Gems of Piety in Humble Life. By the Rev. T. H. WALKER. Royal 18mo. Eight Page Illustrations.

PRICE TWO SHILLINGS.

The Great Apostle; or, Pictures from the Life of St. Paul. By Rev. JABEZ MARRAT. Foolscap 8vo. Twenty-eight Illustrations and Map.

Homes and Home Life in Bible Lands. By J. R. S. CLIFFORD. Foolscap 8vo. Eighty Illustrations.

PRICE TWO SHILLINGS—*continued.*

Martin Luther, the Prophet of Germany. By the Rev. J. SHAW BANKS. Foolscap 8vo. Thirteen Illustrations.

Eminent Christian Philanthropists. Brief Biographical Sketches, designed especially as Studies for the Young. By the Rev. GEORGE MAUNDER. Foolscap 8vo.

Peter Pengelly; or, 'True as the Clock.' By J. JACKSON WRAY. Crown 8vo. Forty Illustrations.

The Tower, the Temple, and the Minster: Historical and Biographical Associations of the Tower of London, St. Paul's Cathedral, and Westminster Abbey. By the Rev. J. W. THOMAS. Foolscap 8vo. Six Steel Engravings.

Youthful Obligations. Illustrated by a large number of Appropriate Facts and Anecdotes. Foolscap 8vo. With Illustrations.

Hid Treasures, and the Search for Them: being Lectures to Bible Classes. By the Rev. JOHN HARTLEY. Foolscap 8vo.

PRICE EIGHTEENPENCE.

'Little Ray' Series. Royal 16mo.

Little Ray and Her Friends. By RUTH ELLIOTT. Five Page Illustrations.

The History of the Tea-Cup; with a Descriptive Account of the Potter's Art. By the Rev. G. R. WEDGWOOD. Profusely Illustrated.

The Cliftons, and their Play-Hours. By Mrs. COSSLETT. Seven Page Illustrations.

Ned's Motto; or, Little by Little. By the Author of 'Faithful and True,' 'Tony Starr's Legacy.' Six Page Illustrations.

The Bear's Den. By E. H. MILLER. Six Page Illustrations.

Broken Purposes; or, the Good Time Coming. By LILLIE MONTFORT. Five page Illustrations.

The Breakfast Half-Hour. Addresses on Religious and Moral Topics. By the Rev. H. R. BURTON. Twenty-five Illustrations.

Gleanings in Natural History for Young People. Profusely Illustrated.

The Stony Road: A Tale of Humble Life.

'Wee Donald:' Sequel to 'Stony Road.'

Stories for Willing Ears. For Boys. By T. S. E.

Stories for Willing Ears. For Girls. By T. S. E.

Thirty Thousand Pounds: and other Sketches from Daily Life.

An Old Sailor's Yarn: and other Sketches from Daily Life.

The Royal Road to Riches. By E. H. MILLER. Fifteen Illustrations.

PRICE EIGHTEENPENCE. *Foolscap 8vo. Series.*

David Livingstone, Missionary and Discoverer. By the Rev. J. MARRAT. Fifteen Page Illustrations.

PRICE EIGHTEENPENCE. *Foolscap 8vo. Series—continued.*

Memorable Men and Memorable Events. By GEORGE CUBITT. Numerous Illustrations. Price 1s. 6d. each.

1. COLUMBUS; or, The Discovery of America.
2. CORTES; or, The Discovery and Conquest of Mexico.
3. PIZARRO; or, The Discovery and Conquest of Peru.
4. GRANADA; or, The Expulsion of the Moors from Spain.

Three Indian Heroes: the Missionary; the Soldier; the Statesman. By the Rev. J. SHAW BANKS. Second Edition. Numerous Illustrations.

Old Truths in New Lights. Illustrations of Scripture Truth for the Young. By W. H. S. Numerous Illustrations.

The Father of Methodism. A Sketch of the Life and Labours of the Rev. John Wesley, A.M. For Young People. By Mrs. COSSLETT. Second Edition, enlarged. Numerous Illustrations.

Chequer Alley: A Story of Successful Christian Work. By the Rev. FREDERICK W. BRIGGS, M.A. Eleventh Edition.

Home: or, The Way to Make Home Happy. By the Rev. DAVID HAY. 18mo., gilt edges.

PRICE ONE SHILLING AND FOURPENCE.

The Boatman's Daughter. A Narrative for the Learned and the Unlearned. By the Rev. ALFRED BARRETT. 18mo. With Frontispiece.

PRICE ONE SHILLING.

Royal 16mo. Numerous Illustrations.

Rob Rat; A Story of Barge Life. By MARK GUY PEARSE. Numerous Illustrations.

The Tarnside Evangel. By M. A. H. Eight Illustrations.

Robert Dawson; or, The Brave Spirit. Four Page Illustrations.

The Meadow Daisy. By LILLIE MONTFORT. Numerous Illustrations.

The Unwelcome Baby, and what Became of Him; with other Stories of noble Lives Early Consecrated. By S. ELLEN GREGORY. Nine Illustrations.

'I'll Try;' or, How the Farmer's Son became a Captain. Ten Illustrations.

The Royal Disciple: Louisa, Queen of Prussia. By C. R. HURST. Six Illustrations.

No Gains without Pains: A True Life for the Boys. By H. C. KNIGHT. Six Illustrations.

The Railway Pioneers; or, The Story of the Stephensons, Father and Son. By H. C. KNIGHT. Fifteen Illustrations.

Peeps into the Far North: Chapters on Iceland, Lapland, and Greenland. By S. E. SCHOLES. Twenty-four Illustrations.

The Giants, and How to Fight Them. By Dr. RICHARD NEWTON. Fifteen Illustrations.

Stories of Love and Duty. For Boys and Girls. Thirty-one Illustrations.

PRICE ONE SHILLING—*continued.*

John Tregenoweth; His Mark. By MARK GUY PEARSE. Twenty-five Illustrations.

Vignett from English History. By the Rev. JAMES YEAMES. First Series. From the Norman Conqueror to Henry IV. Twenty-three Illustrations.

Margery's Christmas Box. By RUTH ELLIOTT. Seven Illustrations.

Tiny Tim: A Story of London Life. Founded on Fact. By FRANCIS HORNER. Twenty-two Illustrations.

Lessons from Noble Lives, and other Stories. Thirty-one Illustrations.

Ancient Egypt: Its Monuments, Worship, and People. By the Rev. EDWARD LIGHTWOOD. Twenty-six Illustrations.

William the Silent, Prince of Orange. A Biographical Sketch. By the Rev. J. W. THOMAS. Foolscap 8vo. With Portrait.

Helen Leslie; or, Truth and Error. By ADELINE. 18mo.

Sketches from my Schoolroom. By the Daughter of a Wesleyan Minister. 18mo. Four Illustrations.

Life on the Waves; or, Memorials of Captain George LEONARD. By the Rev. A. LANGLEY. With Illustrations. 18mo.

PRICE NINEPENCE. 18mo.

Dick's Troubles; and How He Met Them. By RUTH ELLIOTT. Six Illustrations.

The Wonderful Lamp; and other Stories. By RUTH ELLIOTT, Five Illustrations.

Ragged Jim's Last Song; and other Ballads. By EDWARD BAILEY. Eight Illustrations.

Rosa's Christmas Invitations; and other Stories. By LILLIE MONTFORT. Six Illustrations.

Nora Grayson's Dream; and other Stories. By LILLIE MONTFORT. Seven Illustrations.

The Chat in the Meadow: and other Stories. By LILLIE MONTFORT. Six Illustrations.

John's Teachers: and other Stories. By LILLIE MONTFORT. Six Illustrations.

Pictures from Memory. By ADELINE. Nine Illustrations.

The Story of the Wreck of the 'Maria' Mail Boat: with a Memoir of Mrs. Hincksman, the only Survivor. Illustrated.

Passages from the Life of Heinrich Stilling. Five Page Illustrations.

The above are sold in Limp Cloth at EIGHTPENCE.

PRICE EIGHTPENCE.

Precious Seed, and Little Sowers. 18mo. Four Illustrations. Gilt edges.

Janie: A Flower from South Africa. By Rev. R. LAMPLOUGH. 18mo. With Portrait.

Freddie Cleminson: The Brief Story of a Blessed Life. By the Rev. T. M'CULLAGH. 18mo. With Portrait, &c.

PRICE EIGHTPENCE—*continued.*

Soon and Safe: A Word to the Young Folks. By Rev. SIMPSON CRUMP. 18mo. Illustrations.

Christianity Compared with Popery: A Lecture.

Death of the Eldest Son. By CÆSAR MALAN.

Emily's Lessons; or, Chapters in the Life of a Young Christian.

Fragments for Young People.

History of Joseph. By AGNES BULMER.

Jonathan Saville's Life. By the Rev. F. A. WEST.

The Sunday Scholar's Guide. By the Rev. J. T. BARR.

PRICE SIXPENCE.

Cloth, Illuminated, and Coloured Frontispiece.

1. A Kiss for a Blow: Stories about Peace and War.
2. Louis Henrie; or, The Sister's Promise.
3. The Giants, and How to Fight Them. By Dr. RICHARD NEWTON.
4. Robert Dawson; or, the Brave Spirit.
5. Jane Hudson, the American Girl.
6. The Jewish Twins. By AUNT FRIENDLY.
7. The Book of Beasts. Thirty-five Illustrations.
8. The Book of Birds. Forty Illustrations.
9. Proud in Spirit.
10. Althea Norton.
11. Gertrude's Bible Lesson.
12. The Rose in the Desert.
13. The Little Black Hen.
14. Martha's Hymn.
15. Nettie Mathieson.
16. The Prince in Disguise.
17. The Children of the Plains.
18. The Babes in the Basket.
19. Richard Harvey; or, Taking a Stand.
20. Kitty King: Lessons for Little Girls.
21. Nettie's Mission.
22. Little Margery.
23. Margery's City Home.
24. The Crossing Sweeper.
25. Rosy Conroy's Lessons.
26. Ned Dolan's Garret.
27. Little Henry and his Bearer.
28. Little Woodman and his Dog Cæsar.

The above are sold in Ornamental Stiff Covers at FOURPENCE *each.*

Hattie and Nancy; or, The Everlasting Love. With Illustrations. 18mo. Cloth, gilt-lettered, 6d. (A BOOK FOR GIRLS.)

Michael Faraday. By W. R. BURGESS. With Portrait and Illustrations. 18mo. Cloth, gilt-lettered, 6d. (A BOOK FOR BOYS.)

WESLEYAN CONFERENCE OFFICE,
2, CASTLE-STREET, CITY-ROAD; AND 66, PATERNOSTER-ROW.